STRATEGIC PLANNING IN BUSINESS AND GOVERNMENT

STRATEGIC PLANNING IN BUSINESS AND GOVERNMENT

MICHAEL H. MOSKOW

COMMITTEE FOR ECONOMIC DEVELOPMENT

The Committee for Economic Development is an independent research and educational organization of two hundred business men and educators. CED is nonprofit, nonpartisan, and nonpolitical and is supported by contributions from business, foundations, and individuals. Its objective is to promote stable growth with rising living standards and increasing opportunities for all.

All CED policy recommendations must be approved by the Research and Policy Committee, a group of sixty trustees, which alone can speak for the organization. In issuing statements on national policy, CED often publishes background papers deemed worthy of wider circulation because of their contribution to the understanding of a public problem. This study relates to *Improving Federal Program Performance* (1971). It has been approved for publication as supplementary paper number 41 by an editorial board of trustees and advisors. It also has been read by the members of the Research Advisory Board, who have the right to submit individual memoranda of comment for publication.

While publication of this supplementary paper is authorized by CED's bylaws, except as noted above its contents have not been approved, disapproved, or acted upon by the Committee for Economic Development, the Board of Trustees, the Research and Policy Committee, the Research Advisory Board, the research staff, or any member of any board or committee, or any officer of CED.

Library of Congress Cataloging in Publication Data

Moskow, Michael H.
    Strategic planning in business and government.

    (A Supplementary paper of the Committee for Economic Development; 41)
    1. Corporate planning—United States. 2. Administrative agencies—Planning—United States. I. Title.
HD30.28.M66   658.4'01   78-23401
ISBN 0-87186-241-7

First Printing: December 1978

Printed in the United States of America

Price: $3.50

Committee for Economic Development
477 Madison Avenue, New York, N.Y. 10022

TABLE OF CONTENTS

Foreword   vii

Preface   ix

1.
Planning in Private Industry   1
What is Corporate Planning?   1
Common Elements of Corporate Planning   4
Strategic vs. Operational Planning   6
Examples of Corporate Planning   7
       General Electric Company   7
       The IBM Corporation   8
       Ford Motor Company   9
       Manufacturers Hanover Trust Company   10

2.
Planning in the Federal Government   12
Planning in Cabinet Departments   19
Planning at the Bureau Level   21
       Bureau of Standards   22
       Federal Bureau of Prisons   23
       National Park Service   23
Strategic and Operational Planning   24

3.
The Unique Environment of Government   26
Separation of Powers and Checks and Balances   27
Lack of Profit Motive   30
Periodic Leadership Turnover   31
A Note on Definitions   33

4.
Findings and Conclusions   36
What is Planning?   36
Lack of a Corporate Planning Model   37
Lack of Transferability to Government   38
Importance of Planning in Government   39
Setting Goals and Performance Objectives   40
Role of Program Evaluation   41
Diverse Planning Systems   42
Involvement of Top Management   43

Planning and Implementation   43
Thorough Environmental Understanding   44
A Continuing Dialogue   45

Appendix   46
Case Studies   46
    General Electric Company   46
    The IBM Corporation   50
    Ford Motor Company   55
    Manufacturers Hanover Trust Company   62
    National Bureau of Standards   65
    Federal Bureau of Prisons   73
    National Park Service   76

About the Author   86

FOREWORD

For the past several years a major research focus of the Committee for Economic Development has been directed towards "Improving the Long-Term Performance of the U.S. Economy." Our activities in this field encompass a broad spectrum of related studies on significant long-range economic problems and the appropriate role of government in dealing with them. Individual projects now underway or being initiated include studies concerned with assessing the role and magnitude of regulation and government intervention in the economy, developing criteria for judging the appropriateness of such intervention, improving government organization for economic policy decision making, and analysis of the policy implications of an increasing international economic interdependence. Other studies on energy, technology policy, and urban problems are being closely integrated with the broader project on economic performance. CED is grateful to The Andrew W. Mellon Foundation for its support of this major undertaking, of which *Strategic Planning in Business and Government* is a part.

As a consequence of the emergence of new economic problems such as energy, and the intractability of the old problems of growth, inflation, and employment, there are strong pressures for more disciplined government policy making that anticipates change. The influence of government on the economy is so profound and has so many facets that it is crucial to take a more systematic view of government decision making, in choosing intervention points, coordinating interrelated programs, and predicting the consequences of government action.

As one part of CED's exploration of this subject, Michael H. Moskow was commissioned to undertake a selective survey comparing planning in federal domestic policy making with planning in business. The purpose of the survey was to determine to what extent corporate planning processes may be applicable to government. As Dr. Moskow notes, two key assumptions underlie this study: "First is the belief that better planning leads to more rational decision making and better government policies and programs; and second, that better government policies provide an improved environment for . . . business, labor, agriculture, and the consumer." Thus the study focuses on business and government planning as a process of improving decisions — as to objectives and priorities, as to means of achieving objectives and priorities, and as a way of monitoring and coordinating ongoing programs as a feedback mechanism for future decisions.

It should be emphasized that the study does not deal with national economic planning, nor is it concerned with aspects of modern management techniques other than strategic and operational planning. Government can make much use of improved management techniques, and a number of those have already been well tested within corporations (e.g., cost-benefit analysis, project budgeting, discounted cash flow, and performance-based employee compensation), but this study focuses on one feature only — the potential for transferring corporate strategic and operational planning techniques to government agencies.

This report is intended to provide supporting information and analysis for the ongoing work of CED's Subcommittees on "Improving the Long-Term Performance of the U.S. Economy" and "Regulation and the Role of Government Intervention in the Economy." It is published as a CED supplementary paper in the belief that it will also be of interest to a wider audience. The conclusions expressed in this paper represent solely the opinion of the author and in no way reflect CED's views.

Robert C. Holland
President
Committee for Economic Development

PREFACE

In 1976, the Committee for Economic Development initiated a multi-year study on *Improving the Long-Term Performance of the U. S. Economy.* A major portion of this project will focus on the federal government and its relation to the long-term performance of the economy.

Given the size and the magnitude of federal government activities, improving the performance of government is important to improving the performance of the economy. However, when the potential impact of government policies and regulation on the economy is examined, it becomes even clearer that improving the performance of government is a crucial ingredient in this overall goal.

The activities of the federal government directly affect the economic processes in our country. Governmental functions include economic stabilization, regulation of business and labor, social welfare, national defense, and the production of goods and services. In addition, the federal government provides the legal context within which economic relations take place.

Both Congress and federal executive agencies make major policy decisions that affect the economic environment for business and consumers. To mention a few obvious examples, tax policy affects the distribution of income and provides incentives or disincentives for investment in certain industries; monetary and fiscal policies affect the rate of growth of the economy; and energy policy determines the structure of industrial production and seriously affects life styles.

The role of the Executive Branch in implementing programs is of major importance. Government programs that regulate air and water quality, product safety, pensions and the safety and health of employees, for example, have a substantial impact on the economic calculus underlying business decisions to build and design plants and products. In 1976, over 3,000 new federal regulations were issued. Government agencies distribute billions of dollars to individuals through social security and grant-in-aid programs. The government also provides a wide variety of services, such as employment exchange and various types of insurance to producers and consumers in our economy.

One mechanism which has been advocated to improve the performance of government is to improve the planning that takes place before government acts. There are two key assumptions that underlie this proposal. First is the belief that better planning leads to more rational decision making and better government policies and programs; and second, that better government policies provide an improved environment for the key sectors in our economy: business, labor, agriculture, and the consumer. With this in mind CED initiated a project in February 1977 to review planning activities by business firms to determine whether such processes and techniques would be useful to government. What, if anything, can government learn from the experiences that private business firms have had with corporate planning?

CED appointed the author as project director and an advisory committee in February 1977. All members of the committee had extensive experience in private industry and represented a broad cross-section of industries. In order to provide a broader view of corporate planning and its use in private industry, committee members consisted of both planners and "users" of planning. The committee met with federal government officials in the course of its work. In addition, the author had experience at the policy-making level in four federal government agencies.

The project focused on analyzing the characteristics, needs, and processes of business and government planning. The research and analysis focused mainly on large business firms and federal agencies with domestic policy concerns. Specifically excluded were the Department of Defense, the State Department, and the National Security Council, where formal planning appears to have developed to a larger extent than in agencies focusing on domestic policy. As part of the background work for the project, the author reviewed the literature on corporate planning and made field trips to eight companies in order to study a broad spectrum of approaches to corporate planning. Whenever possible, "users" of planning in these companies were interviewed to obtain their views of the planning process. Planning processes in three different government agencies were reviewed intensively. In addition, government officials and former government officials who had experience in private industry were interviewed.

The difficulties encountered in the study centered on the scope of the project and the definition of concepts. As will be discussed later in more detail, private industry is large and diverse; both characteristics also apply to the federal government, making analysis of the two sectors extremely complex. Even more difficult, however, is defining the concept of "planning." Although the term "planning" is widely used, it is subject to greatly differing interpretation even by individuals within the same industry, company, or government agency. Moreover, there is no commonly accepted definition or terminology in the academic literature. In addition, planning is difficult to separate from other management functions such as policy making and budgeting.

"Planning" is also an emotion-laden term so that serious discussion is sometimes made difficult. To some, "planning" connotes "rational thought," and that meaning leads to support for the use of planning by any individual or organization, including the federal government. Others immediately infer that any planning in government is the kind of "national planning" or "national economic planning" that implies production, price and other types of controls, and should, therefore, be opposed. A range of other views also exists.

This project focused on the use of planning to improve the government's performance in both its policy-making and program-implementation roles. It did not include the kind of "national planning" that entails decisions by government on how resources are to be allocated, what goods and services are to be produced, and how they are to be distributed.

The author would like to express his appreciation to David L. Grove, IBM Corporation, and Charles B. Stauffacher,

Field Enterprises, Inc., who served as trustee advisors and to the following persons who served on the Advisory Committee:

Michael G. Allen
General Electric Company

Walter A. Couper
Federated Department Stores, Inc.

David B. Elkin
W. R. Grace & Co., Inc.

Robert C. Isban
Manufacturers Hanover Trust Company

Douglas G. G. Levick, III
IBM Corporation

John M. Stewart (Chairman)
McKinsey & Company, Inc.

Robert C. White
Ford Motor Company

The author assumes complete responsibility for the analysis and conclusions in this report, but he received invaluable assistance from the trustee advisors and the Advisory Committee without whose support the project could not have been completed in the time allotted. The views expressed herein are solely those of the author and not Esmark, Inc., of which he is vice president for corporate development and planning. The author is particularly grateful to Shawn Bernstein, who researched and wrote the government case studies and helped the author think through this complex subject.

Strategic Planning in Business and Government

1

PLANNING IN PRIVATE INDUSTRY

Planning is an extremely difficult concept to define. Viewed broadly, it is a process of deciding what to do and how to do it before some action is taken. Using this broad definition, of course, almost any decision involves some planning. Despite the fact that management textbooks include "planning" as one of the main functions of a manager at any level of an organization, "planning" is very hard to define and describe in a rigorous and complete fashion.

WHAT IS CORPORATE PLANNING?

Formal strategic planning in business is a relatively new activity which emerged on a wide-scale basis during the last fifteen years. An increasing number of large companies are utilizing formal corporate planning systems that often encompass five-year and one-year time frames. This type of regular planning for predetermined time periods is sometimes called "period planning" as distinguished from planning for a specific project or program. Companies have initiated planning systems because of the increasing complexity of their organizations and the increasing complexity of the environment in which they operate.

Planning is a more amorphous function than finance,

marketing, or employee relations. The activities included under the rubric of corporate planning are subject to a wide amount of discretion by the Chief Executive Officer (CEO) and other top managers in the organization. In fact, the management style of the CEO and other top officials appears to be the most important determinant of corporate planning functions and activities. Corporate planning tends to reflect the specific needs and requirements of top management, and its activities are not dependent on groups outside the organization.

Corporate planning activities also vary by corporate size and structure. Larger companies tend to have a more formal corporate planning system with a separate member of the management team having full-time responsibility for planning. Highly decentralized companies often use corporate planning as a major element in their system of communications and management control. In some companies the planning official reports to the chief financial officer; in others he reports directly to the CEO. In large multi-product companies, corporate planning tends to focus more on financial matters, particularly capital expenditure decisions. In smaller companies and in large single-product companies, top management often becomes more involved in the details of production processes, marketing strategies, and distribution systems. Corporate planning reflects this tendency. Capital intensive businesses tend to utilize planning more extensively because of the high risks involved in major capital expenditures and because the obvious competition between alternative capital expenditures seems amenable to a disciplined approach.

As with all corporate officials, the way the CEO views the corporate planner and the confidence and trust he places in him are important determinants of the influence the planner has within the company. In some cases, a corporate planner will be deeply involved in major corporate decisions, not because of the planning system, but because of his personal relationship with the CEO. Using exactly the same planning system, that planner's successor probably would not have the same degree of influence. It is important not to confuse the personal influence of a planner with the success of a corporate planning system.

Planning is a process that must be tailored to the unique characteristics of the organization in which it is carried out. As discussed earlier, the style of management and the structure of the organization are among the more important determinants of the type of planning conducted at various levels within the organization. It is common parlance within corporate planning circles that a planning system cannot be transferred from one company to another without modifying it to meet the unique environment in which it will operate.

The planning system within a firm must also change over time to reflect the firm's mix of businesses or product lines. Key management decision makers change as well, and the planning system must adapt to their personalities and management styles. In general, planning differs between companies and within companies over time. Planning is unique to a particular company at a given point in time and with given personnel.

The academic literature on corporate planning is extensive. Hundreds of articles and books have been written on the subject, and it is commonly included in the curriculum in schools of business administration. Unfortunately, this vast body of literature provides no commonly accepted definition or basic concepts of corporate planning. In general, the academic literature does not reflect the complexity of the business environment.

A number of research studies, often using different definitions, have attempted to assess the impact of corporate planning. Although many companies use corporate planning extensively, few of these studies have found evidence that corporate planning is associated with successful business operations or higher profits. This does not mean, of course, that planning is not associated with higher profits, only that these research studies have not found conclusive evidence to that effect.*

---

*See for example: Murray Weidenbaum and Linda Rockwood, "Corporate Planning Versus Government Planning," *Public Interest*, Winter 1977; Peter Lorange, "Formal Planning Systems — The State of the Art," Working Paper, Sloan School of Management, M.I.T., October 1974; and David W. Ewing, *The Human Side of Planning, Tool or Tyrant?* (New York, Macmillan & Co., 1969.)

In fairness to these studies, however, it should be emphasized that corporate planning is an extremely difficult subject to research because it is so dependent on management style and company and industry variations. It may be a subject that cannot be explored adequately given the current state of the art of research methodology. Furthermore, corporate planning often includes information that is highly confidential because it focuses on competitive assessments and strategies. Companies have a vested interest in making it appear to their stockholders, potential investors, and financial analysts that they have a highly systematic approach to corporate planning even though in practice the planning system may provide little assistance in company operations.

COMMON ELEMENTS OF CORPORATE PLANNING

After reviewing the experiences of a number of private companies, five common elements of corporate planning appear to be particularly important:

1. Setting goals or objectives

2. Assessing and forecasting the external environment, such as economic growth, inflation rates, changes in government regulation, exchange rates, actions of foreign governments, etc.

3. Designing and assessing alternative courses of action, including an analysis of the potential risks and rewards

4. Selecting the best course of action

5. Evaluating results as the course of action is implemented (commonly called "control")

Planning is an interactive process that usually includes these five elements, although a formal integrated planning system is not always utilized. At times, planning takes place in an *ad hoc* informal fashion which may include the CEO spending an hour thinking through the problem, making a decision, and establishing a simple reporting requirement. A brainstorming session of several top executives may be used to accomplish the same objective. At the other extreme is the company with a full-time Director of Corporate Planning who coordinates a formal, highly articulated planning system.

Planning must be dynamic in order for it to be effective. The external environment in which an organization operates is constantly changing in a highly unpredictable manner. Since no one can accurately predict the future, the plans that result from corporate planning must be changed as external events alter the balance of risks and rewards of various options.

Planning includes a long-range assessment, but it focuses on decisions and actions for the near term. In some companies, forecasting external events or "horizon scanning" is sometimes called "planning." These activities are part of the process of planning as here defined, but unless they are conducted within a decision-making framework, they are not considered "planning" in this study.

The above five elements distinguish corporate planning from the broad definition of planning, deciding in advance what to do, discussed earlier. Particularly important are the first element, setting goals and objectives, and the last, evaluation. If goals are established, together with a feedback mechanism that measures progress and continually modifies courses of action to accomplish these goals, planning becomes a process of management as opposed to merely thinking in advance about future problems. Precisely how these activities are carried out within a business firm, of course, will vary greatly depending on management style, industry, personalities, organizational structure, and tradition.

Firms often establish a three- or five-year planning system that is tied to the firm's one-year budget cycle. The early phases of planning are devoted to the longer term strategic issues while the latter phases focus on the immediate year ahead. In the process a one-year budget including projections of sales, costs, earnings, etc., is prepared which is then utilized to compare with actual results on a monthly basis during the budget year.

STRATEGIC VS. OPERATIONAL PLANNING

Although practices vary, a distinction is often made between strategic and operational planning. Strategic planning focuses on the broad policy questions facing an organization, such as its basic mission and purposes and alternative courses of action or strategies to achieve those missions and purposes. For example, what products should a company produce? What market share should a company seek, and what course of action will be followed to achieve that objective?

Although companies differ depending on their size, every organization makes strategic decisions. Strategic decisions may involve billions of dollars in large companies and thousands of dollars in smaller companies, but within the context of the smaller company, the ten thousand dollar decision could be extremely important.

In a multi-project company, strategic decision making takes place at different levels within the firm. At the corporate level, assessing the portfolio of businesses or product lines and possible acquisitions or divestitures are major strategic decisions. At the division level, the strategic decisions focus more on the health and growth of the businesses in which the company is already engaged. Finally, the department level will focus more on decisions related to marketing programs, production programs, and so on.

Operational planning is more limited in its range of concerns, and it usually focuses on problems of implementing broader goals or objectives that have already been determined. It is often the plan for a specific function, such as marketing, production, or new plant construction.

The distinction between strategic and operational planning is sometimes blurred. In most cases, however, strategic planning is conducted at higher levels of management, includes a larger range of alternatives, covers a longer period of time, and includes a higher degree of uncertainty and more unstructured problems. In addition, strategic planning takes a corporate-wide perspective, while operational planning is done principally from a functional or suborganizational point of view.

The process of strategic planning forces management to identify and address its major decisions in an analytical and systematic manner. Goals are often set and communicated throughout the organization as part of the process. As a by-product, management develops a deeper understanding of its business and the environment in which it is operating. In fact, many planners believe that the process and discipline of strategic planning is far more important than the final product or "plan."

EXAMPLES OF CORPORATE PLANNING

In order to provide a better understanding of corporate planning activities, four case studies are included in Appendix A. These studies examine the General Electric Company, the IBM Corporation, Ford Motor Company, and Manufacturers Hanover Trust Company.

The case studies were prepared by the firms. They are not based on observation by the author of the actual planning process. The cases illustrate the diversity of corporate planning processes. They also provide insights into the ways corporate planning is integrated into different management structures. In addition, the cases illustrate the relationship between different types of planning and control systems.

GENERAL ELECTRIC COMPANY

The General Electric Company is a $17 billion highly diversified manufacturing company. Through its different products it competes with over eighty of the top 200 industrial corporations in the United States.

General Electric's approach to planning is highly decentralized, with strategy development carried out below the corporate level. The company is divided into 44 strategic business units each of which prepares a strategic plan annually. A corporate plan is developed which shapes the overall corporate direction and priorities — against which business units can develop their own strategies.

The company has an annual planning cycle which starts with long-range strategies and then fits its short-range operating goals to them. The strategies of most of the 44 business units are reviewed in depth within this cycle. Selectivity is required, and certain business units are given more or less attention each year.

The managerial environment in General Electric stresses balance of near-term financial results with future development. The case study describes how compensation increases and how bonuses are based on factors that benefit the business in the future instead of being solely based on current year's performance.

THE IBM CORPORATION

The IBM Corporation is a $16 billion business machine manufacturing firm that receives about one-half of its revenues from outside the United States. Activities are grouped into a number of operating units which, where feasible, have profit and loss responsibility. The planning and control system pervades the entire organizational structure and serves as a primary communication link between corporate and operating unit management. The planning system establishes unit objectives and strategic direction, negotiates plan commitments, and measures performance against plan. Planning and implementation are line management responsibilities with support provided by planning staffs at the corporate, operating unit, and plant or laboratory level.

IBM has two general categories of planning: program planning and period planning. Plans to develop a product or improve the productivity of a function are called program planning. The time horizons for a program plan are determined by the nature of specific program objectives and the work processes required to achieve it. At any point in time, each operating unit has a large portfolio of product and functional programs in various stages of planning and implementation.

Period planning, in which time horizons are fixed by corporate management, includes both strategic and operating plans. Each operating unit annually performs both strategic and operating planning. The purpose of strategic planning is to establish a unit's business direction; operating planning implements the direction within budgeting requirements and commits the unit to achieving planned results. Corporate management assigns targets (profit and profit margin) to each operating unit. Each operating unit management then develops and assigns goals to its product/system and functional management to guide their strategy development.

In order to help deal with the problems of uncertainty, corporate management may request contingency analyses to test the effect of, for example, a more extreme set of economic assumptions on unit plans. The company's economists may issue two outlooks, one for the base plan, and a second for the contingency plan. Operating units will then develop two plans and review them with corporate management.

FORD MOTOR COMPANY

The Ford Motor Company, a $29 billion company, is the second largest automobile manufacturer in the United States. In the past, Ford has had no formal "planning office" that has as its sole and complete duty the development and administration of long-range plans. As an evolutionary step, however, Ford is in the process of establishing an organization to integrate strategic and business plans and of extending its planning horizons; accordingly, the planning process described herein is historic in nature.

The central staffs play a major role in developing goals for the company and its various components. The staffs also review specific plans developed by the operating units and maintain reports designed to measure progress toward objectives. The basic formulation of plans, however, remains the responsibility of the operating divisions.

Ford has selected two principal goals: (1) to increase substantially (by a designated amount) its profits per share in the next few years; and (2) to reach an objective (and specified) rate of return on assets. The second goal, rate of return on assets, is established for each of Ford's divisions and subsidiaries, which are called "profit centers."

The goals are reviewed annually under the direction of the office of the Chief Executive. If warranted, the goals are changed. The central staffs coordinate the establishment and dissemination of several fiscal policies, population trends, productivity rates, and so on. These assumptions are communicated to divisional planners for use in developing their plans.

Ford develops several separate sets of plans. The "product plan" includes its package size, functional characteristics, styling, investment, and piece cost. Each division prepares a plan that includes a detailed budget for the next year and plans for the succeeding four years in more general outline form. The "research plan" is a systematic statement of assignments, time frames for reports, and decisions that must be made with regard to the reports. The studies include scientific and technical research as well as long-range economic and market analyses. "Supplementary plans" are primarily nonfinancial and focus on subjects such as management development, product quality, and supplies.

MANUFACTURERS HANOVER TRUST COMPANY

Manufacturers Hanover Trust Company is a large multibillion dollar bank holding company consisting of several affiliated banks and bank-related subsidiaries. Manufacturers Hanover's approach to planning includes two interrelated phases: the five-year strategic plan and the one-year profit plan which includes a major expenditure management system and quarterly management reviews.

The purpose of the five-year strategic plan is to identify the components of the near- and long-term earnings flows and to help insure that these flows are at optimal levels. The written support document's purpose is to develop awareness of the internal and external factors influencing the future of the corporation.

The one-year profit plan has a higher level of detail and

greater tactical emphasis. It includes detailed proposals for revenues and expense as well as sources and use of funds. It outlines specific programs to be implemented by the business unit during the year, in line with the strategies presented in its five-year plan.

For the profit plan, variance analyses against actual performance are developed to track progress and to make appropriate operating changes. These variances are reviewed quarterly and presented to senior management at Quarterly Management Review Meetings. Variances from the plan for the entire year, based on preliminary financial information, are reviewed each December, and the following year's profit plan is presented to senior management.

Manufacturers Hanover has a corporate planning department which assists in the development of formal divisional and departmental plans throughout the organization. Each division, department, subsidiary, and affiliate has a designated corporate planning coordinator whose role is to organize the unit plans. He develops, with senior management, overall divisional goals and strategies for the five-year strategic plan. In addition, he assists units within the division in developing new products and services, monitoring specific projects, and providing management with progress reports on implementation of strategies.

2

PLANNING IN THE FEDERAL GOVERNMENT

Of the three branches of the federal government — Legislative, Executive and Judiciary — most formal planning takes place within the Executive Branch. This branch consists of cabinet level departments, subcabinet level bureaus, and the White House and the Executive Office of the President. Policy making and planning take place at all levels. In almost all cases, Congress has enacted specific legislation creating agencies and later providing funds for their operation. The independent regulatory agencies, such as the Civil Aeronautics Board (CAB), Federal Trade Commission (FTC), and Federal Communications Commission (FCC), are not part of the Executive Branch, although the President appoints the chairmen and members with the advice and consent of the Senate.

The key staff members serving the President are housed in the White House or the Executive Office of the President, which includes the Office of Management and Budget (OMB). Staff members often head or coordinate interagency task forces that address specific policy issues such as energy, crime, and drug abuse. The OMB establishes preliminary guidelines and reviews all budget requests from agency heads and takes responsibility for assembling the President's budget request to Congress. OMB staff also attempts to coordinate program evaluation activities of the agencies. In recent administrations,

OMB has coordinated and encouraged various management systems, such as Program Planning Budgeting Systems (PPBS), Management by Objectives (MBO), and currently, Zero Base Budgeting (ZBB). Other staff groups in the Executive Office of the President have included: Congressional Affairs, Public Affairs, National Security Council staff, Domestic Policy staffs, and liaisons with states, cities, and special groups. The number and scope of staff group responsibilities vary depending on the operating style of the President.

In recent years, presidents have established special groups to coordinate policy making for high priority areas. President Carter, for example, has formed an Economic Policy Group (EPG) headed by the Secretary of the Treasury and consisting of the Chairman of the Council of Economic Advisers, the Director of OMB, and cabinet secretaries whose departments include activities relevant to economic policy. President Ford established a similar group to achieve coordination in areas of economic policy.

The major organizational units within the Executive Branch are the thirteen cabinet departments. Noncabinet agencies include the Veterans Administration, Equal Employment Opportunity Commission, Environmental Protection Agency, and the Small Business Administration. Each cabinet-level department is a grouping of bureaus that often perform widely varying functions and employ persons with different types of skills. Table 1, on page 14, shows the total range of federal government functions by budget category. Most bureaus have been created by congressional action which sometimes predates the establishment of the cabinet department within which it resides, especially in the case of the newer cabinet agencies such as the Department of Health, Education and Welfare (1953), the Department of Housing and Urban Development (1965), the Department of Transportation (1966), and the Department of Energy (1977). Table 2 (pages 15-18) entitled *A Typology of Government Agencies and Programs* provides a broad-brush listing of government agencies and programs by primary function. The list is not comprehensive, but it is illustrative of the broad and varied functions performed by the federal agencies.

Table 1

Federal Government Functions by Budget Category

EDUCATION AND MANPOWER

Elementary and secondary education

Higher education

Vocational education

Manpower training

Other education

Other manpower aids

COMMERCE AND TRANSPORTATION

Air transportation

Water transportation

Ground transportation

U. S. Postal Service

Area and regional development

AGRICULTURE AND RURAL DEVELOPMENT

Farm income stabilization

Rural housing and public facilities

Agricultural land and water resources

Research and other agricultural services

NATURAL RESOURCES AND ENVIRONMENT

Water resources and power

Land management

Minerals

Pollution control and abatement

Recreation

GENERAL GOVERNMENT

Legislative functions

Judicial functions

Executive direction and management

Central fiscal operations

General property and records management

Law enforcement and justice

NATIONAL DEFENSE

Department of Defense military

Military Assistance

Atomic Energy

Defense-related activities

HEALTH

Development of health resources

Providing or financing medical services

Prevention and control of health problems

INCOME SECURITY

Retirement, disability

Unemployment insurance

Public assistance

Social services

VETERANS BENEFITS AND SERVICES

Income security

Education, training, and rehabilitation

Hospital and medical care

INTERNATIONAL AFFAIRS AND FINANCE

Economic and financial assistance

Food for Peace

Other

Space research and technology

Manned space flight

COMMUNITY DEVELOPMENT AND HOUSING

Community planning, management, and development

Low and moderate income housing aids

Maintenance of the housing mortgage market

Table 2

Typology of Government Agencies and Programs*

1. REGULATORY, SINGLE INDUSTRY

Civil Aeronautics Board (CAB)
Commodity Futures Trading Commission
Comptroller of Currency
Federal Aviation Administration (FAA)
Federal Communications Commission (FCC)
Federal Home Loan Bank Board (FHLBB)
Federal Maritime Commission
Federal Power Commission (FPC)
Federal Reserve Board
Food and Drug Administration (FDA)
Interstate Commerce Commission (ICC)
Nuclear Regulatory Commission
Packers and Stockyards Administration
Securities and Exchange Commission

2. REGULATORY, MULTI-INDUSTRY

Agricultural Marketing Service
Animal and Plant Health Inspection Service
Consumer Product Safety Commission (CPSC)
Environmental Protection Agency (EPA)
Equal Employment Opportunity Commission (EEOC)
Federal Energy Administration (FEA)
Federal Trade Commission (FTC)
National Labor Relations Board (NLRB)
Occupational Safety and Health Administration (OSHA)
Office of Federal Contract Compliance Programs (OFCCP)
Patent and Trademark Office
Pension and Welfare Benefit Programs
Wage and Hour Division

3. AGRICULTURAL PRODUCTION AND STABILIZATION

Agricultural Stabilization and Conservation Service
Commodity Credit Corporation

*This typology is a broad-brush attempt to categorize agencies and programs by primary function. Any such categorization is difficult and tends to be somewhat arbitrary, because agencies perform multiple and overlapping functions. The list is not comprehensive, but it is intended to illustrate the broad and varied functions performed by federal agencies.

4. BLOCK GRANT FOR STATE AND/OR LOCAL AGENCIES

Community Development Block Grant Assistance Program (CD)
Comprehensive Employment and Training Act (CETA)
Economic Development Administration (EDA)
Law Enforcement Assistance Administration (LEAA)

5. GRANTS FOR CONSTRUCTION AND/OR OPERATION OF FACILITIES

Federal Highway Administration
Federal Housing Administration
Maritime Administration
Urban Mass Transit Administration (UMPTA)

6. CONTRACTS FOR CONSTRUCTION OF FACILITIES

Bureau of Prisons
General Services Administration (GSA)

7. DIRECT LOANS

Farmers Home Administration
Rural Electrification Administration

8. INSURANCE PROGRAMS

Federal Crime Insurance Program
Federal Crop Insurance Corporation
Federal Deposit Insurance Corporation (FDIC)
Federal Flood Insurance Program
Pension Benefit Guaranty Corporation (PBGC)

9. TRANSFER PAYMENT PROGRAMS

Aid to Families With Dependent Children (AFDC)
Food and Nutrition Service
Medicare
Social Security
Supplemental Security Income Program (SSI)

10. HEALTH CARE SERVICES

Alcohol, Drug Abuse, and Mental Health Administration
Center for Disease Control
Public Health Service

11. SPECIAL GROUP SERVICES

Bureau of Indian Affairs
Veterans Administration
Women's Bureau

12. EDUCATION AND TRAINING

Bureau of Domestic Commerce
Bureau of Health Manpower
Bureau of International Commerce
Extension Service
Farmer Cooperative Service
National Fire Prevention and Control Administration
Office of Education

13. NATURAL RESOURCE MANAGEMENT AND DEVELOPMENT

Bureau of Land Management
Bureau of Mines
Fish and Wildlife Service
Forest Service
Geologic Survey
National Park Service
Soil Conservation Service

14. TRADE AND PROMOTION

Office of Telecommunications
Travel Service

15. COLLECTION AND ANALYSIS OF STATISTICAL DATA

Bureau of the Census
Bureau of Economic Analysis
Bureau of Labor Statistics (BLS)
Economic Research Service
Statistical Reporting Service

16. RESEARCH AND DEVELOPMENT

Agricultural Research Service
Department of Energy (DOE)
National Aeronautics and Space Administration (NASA)
National Institutes of Health (NIH)
National Science Foundation (NSF)

17. LAW ENFORCEMENT

Anti-Trust Division
Civil Rights Division
Criminal Division
Customs Service
Drug Enforcement Administration

Federal Bureau of Investigation (FBI)
Immigration and Naturalization Service
Secret Service
U.S. Attorney's Office

18. REVENUE COLLECTION

Bureau of Alcohol, Tobacco and Firearms
Internal Revenue Service (IRS)

19. DIRECT OPERATING SERVICES

Bureau of Engraving and Printing
Bureau of Government Financial Operations
Bureau of the Mint
Bureau of the Public Debt
Government Printing Office (GPO)

The Department of Labor, which employs almost 15,000 persons and is one of the smallest cabinet agencies, provides a good example of program and employee skill diversity. Its bureaus include such widely varying activities as collection, analysis, and publication of data (Bureau of Labor Statistics); enforcement of minimum wage and maximum hours of work (Wage and Hour Division); examining claims and paying worker compensation benefits to federal employees (Office of Worker Compensation programs); developing and enforcing occupational health and safety standards (Occupational Safety and Health Administration); promoting the welfare of wage-earning women (Women's Bureau); setting standards for fiduciaries and administrators of pension programs (Pension and Welfare Benefit Program); and providing block grants to improve training and employment opportunities for disadvantaged workers to state and local governments (Employment and Training Administration).

The Department administers over 130 special laws and executive orders. Its employee skill needs range from experts on pension funds to scientists knowledgeable about occupational health, attorneys and law enforcement officials, statisticians, actuaries, persons knowledgeable about state and local government, and others.

Planning in cabinet departments takes place within the bureaus as well as within the Office of the Secretary. A reciprocal relationship exists in which policy guidance is provided to operating bureaus by Presidential staff groups and cabinet Secretaries and their staffs. Each bureau then prepares its own detailed plans for program priorities as well as facilities, personnel, budget, and program. These plans are submitted to the Secretary, and in most cases, a Secretarial level planning staff has responsibility for reviewing bureau plans. In addition, they sometimes formulate comprehensive plans for a department-wide perspective.

PLANNING IN CABINET DEPARTMENTS

While planning staffs within the Office of the Secretary of the cabinet departments have grown rapidly in recent years, some agencies still have very limited staffs or none at all. Congress generally accepts the need for these planning offices which contrasts sharply with its views in earlier periods. At one point, the House Committee on Appropriations eliminated departmental planning staffs from five agencies.

As in business, the organizational structure and functions of planning staffs vary depending on the personal priorities of the cabinet officer, his managerial style, and the organizational structure of the department. The Department of Health, Education and Welfare (HEW), which has a budget of over $100 billion and employs over 100,000 persons, has an Assistant Secretary for Planning and Evaluation. He is responsible for coordinating the department's planning system; developing policies or analyzing issues of major concern to the Secretary, such as welfare reform and health insurance; coordinating the department's decentralized research and evaluation program; and administering a research and development budget of about $20 million, which includes several major social experiments. The office has a staff of about 250 persons.

At the Department of Housing and Urban Development (HUD), which has a much smaller budget and employs about

14,000 persons, the Assistant Secretary for Policy Development and Research performs the same functions as his counterpart at HEW and administers the $60 million departmental research and development funds which are centralized. The Department of the Interior has an Assistant Secretary for Program Development and Budget who performs policy development functions and has administrative responsibility for the department's budget. The Department of Labor has an Assistant Secretary for Policy, Evaluation and Research who has responsibility for department-wide policy development and coordination of research and evaluation activities. In all of these examples, the Assistant Secretary is a Presidential appointee who has been confirmed by the Senate.

The activities of the Assistant Secretary and his planning staff vary widely. He may be, for example, the "right-hand man" of the Secretary, and his activities may be primarily centered on those subjects of greatest interest to the Secretary. These may be large-scale projects that require work over long periods of time or short-term, crisis-solving situations so common at the secretarial level. In some cases, the Assistant Secretary is a "Mr. Outside" and devotes most of his time and that of his staff to major legislation, or he works with the White House or other agencies on policy matters. In others, he is a "Mr. Inside" and at the request of the Secretary devotes his efforts to helping manage the department through the internal departmental planning, budget, and management processes. Staff members in the planning offices tend to be analytically oriented, and in general, they have attempted to encourage the use of analysis and quantitative techniques in formulating policy options and evaluating programs.

The planning Assistant Secretary can provide a department-wide perspective on policy issues and on requests for resources by program offices. Having a planning Assistant Secretary enables the Secretary to obtain a second view of a program or request for resources. As in all organizations the operating program office tends to look at its needs from a narrower perspective than the head of the parent organization. Of course, this often places the planning Assistant Secretary in the position of "looking over the shoulder" of the Assistant

Secretaries and bureau heads with operating responsibilities and often leads to conflict.

The planning Assistant Secretary and his staff have become much more involved in the budget cycle and its use as a key planning tool in recent years. The annual budget is an important discipline in government and it is often a tool for forcing policy decisions or making implicit policy decisions. Some planning staffs have attempted to encourage the bureau heads and cabinet officers to undertake long-range planning and to address questions regarding the goals and programs of the agency and its bureaus. The manner in which such multi-year planning is coordinated with the budget cycle varies by agency. The relative responsibilities of the planning staff and the budget office also vary.

PLANNING AT THE BUREAU LEVEL

In order to provide a better understanding of federal planning activities at the bureau level, three case studies representative of current planning processes are included in Appendix A. These studies examine the National Bureau of Standards in the Department of Commerce, the Federal Bureau of Prisons in the Justice Department, and the National Park Service in the Department of the Interior. As indicated, each of these bureaus is part of a different cabinet-level agency that includes many different bureaus.

The case studies were prepared from bureau handbooks and other written descriptions of planning processes and from interviews with bureau officials. They are not based on observation of the actual planning process. The case studies describe the formal planning process which may be different from actual planning practices in these bureaus.

It is important to emphasize that the formal planning process represents only a small spectrum of the total management process in each bureau. Formal planning activities are usually closely linked with the federal budget process and are circumscribed by various legislative and administrative requirements under which each bureau operates. The planning process tends to be unique to each bureau, reflecting the specific needs and requirements imposed by the agency's statutory mission and the operating style of top management personnel. It should also be noted that all planning decisions at the bureau level take place within a political context characterized by bargaining and incremental decision making.

BUREAU OF STANDARDS

The National Bureau of Standards (NBS) was established in 1901 to provide a national system for physical measurement and to provide various services to improve the use of materials and the application of technology. Today the NBS is one of the nation's largest physical science research organizations. Long-range planning at the National Bureau of Standards is focused on the development of alternative program objectives and strategies based on analysis of anticipated conditions in the external environment over a six-year period (e.g., the budgetary climate, probable congressional and administrative actions, etc.) and projections of scientific and technological trends. The long-range planning process is supplemented by program and planning reviews. Four principal review mechanisms are utilized:

1. NBS internal management and planning reviews

2. NBS contracts with the National Academy of Sciences to provide an external review and evaluation of NBS programs

3. Special evaluations of selected program or issue areas by contractor personnel "under the direct program management of the NBS staff"

4. A statutory visiting committee of five members which reports annually to the Secretary of Commerce on the efficiency of NBS scientific work and the condition of its equipment

FEDERAL BUREAU OF PRISONS

The Federal Bureau of Prisons is responsible for the care and custody of persons convicted of federal crimes and sentenced by the courts to serve a period of time incarcerated in a federal penal institution. Long-range planning at the Bureau of Prisons is constrained by the Bureau's lack of control over the number of inmates and types of offenders in its custody, their length of stay, or the geographic distribution of its clientele. In practice, the courts and U. S. attorneys determine the number of prisoners entering custody of the Bureau, and the Parole Board determines the number of prisoners leaving. A central planning effort undertaken by the Bureau entails the development of a ten-year plan to identify goals and alternative strategies for meeting long-range facilities requirements. This planning process includes an analysis of the existing prison population and projected changes in the long-term population, the formulation of objectives concerning basic quality standards for future prison facilities, and the development of capital investment alternatives including consideration of new facilities and the mix of conventional incarceration vis-a-vis community-based programs.

NATIONAL PARK SERVICE

The National Park Service was established in the Department of Interior in 1916 to administer national parks and national monuments for the enjoyment of the public and to protect and conserve the natural environment, historic objects, and wildlife in these areas. Today the national park system consists of over 300 areas (including national parks, national monuments, national recreation areas, and other types of areas) ranging in size from a tenth of an acre lot to parcels of millions of acres that sometimes transcend state boundaries. A major planning effort in the National Park Service is focused on determining the future use and management of these geographic areas.

Park Service policy and various laws provide for public participation at various stages of the planning process. Workshops and meetings are held to inform the public that a plan is being prepared, to solicit information, and to bring to light public concerns, particularly with regard to controversial issues. Once the planning process is underway, informal workshops are held with the planning team and members of the public to acquire information on technical aspects of the plan and matters of existing or potential conflict. Formal meetings are held to provide the public with an opportunity to evaluate various alternatives under consideration and to comment on the content of the analysis. Finally, draft plans are available for public review for a period of at least thirty days prior to an administrative decision.

Park Service planning must also comply with a wide variety of legislative and executive requirements. All planning efforts, for example, must be consistent with the requirements of the National Park Service Organic Act of 1916, the National Historic Preservation Act of 1966, the National Environmental Policy Act of 1969, and eighteen other statutes.

STRATEGIC AND OPERATIONAL PLANNING

Strategic planning for policies takes place at different levels within the Executive Branch. The level at which a policy issue will be considered depends upon institutional and legal responsibilities, the potential resources involved, and the potential consequences of the decision. Strategic planning can be and has been used at the Presidential, cabinet officer, and bureau head level. Planning for reform of the welfare system is an example of strategic planning that has taken place repeatedly in recent years for Presidential policies.

Operational planning can be divided into planning to implement newly enacted programs or policies and planning to implement existing programs or policies. Both types focus mainly on efficiency and scheduling questions. Operational planning accepts the objectives set forth at a higher level and focuses on accomplishing them in the most efficient manner. When the objectives of a statute are not clear or are internally inconsistent, program administrators are required to identify their own objectives, a process which can result in major policy decisions.

Statutes usually provide relatively short time frames for an administrative agency to prepare for implementation. These periods are often characterized by frenzied but extensive planning to hire key personnel, prepare budgets, find office space, and attend to the many details that require planning before an agency is ready to implement a new statute.

Once administrators gain experience with the program, operational planning takes on a more routine cast. It is often tied to the annual budget cycle and directed at establishing performance targets and scheduling actions by the agency. This type of planning is similar to operational planning in private industry, focusing on the "means" to carry out predetermined "ends."

3

THE UNIQUE ENVIRONMENT OF GOVERNMENT

In our democratic society, planning by government takes place within a political milieu. The separation of powers, checks and balances, and periodic elections described below are key factors influencing the political environment. In a democratic political process, strategic planning tends to be much more open than it is in business, with many persons and groups involved. The results become much less predictable. When legislation is involved, for example, 435 members of the House of Representatives and 100 Senators potentially have a voice in the final decision. To a large extent, Congressmen view legislative proposals from the point of view of their local constituents which may not always be optimum for the nation as a whole.

Policy making, the process of deciding on a course of government action, is essentially a bargaining process. Congress, the Executive Branch, and the courts have legal authority to participate in that process. Interest groups, political parties, and the media are noninstitutional participants. Strategic planning is an analytical technique that can become an aspect of policy making, but analysis and rational thought do not necessarily prevail in a political bargaining process. In fact, rationality is sometimes precluded by the political process.

The decision-making process in government is much more open than that which takes place within a private firm, even if the firm is publicly held. In a private company, participation in strategic planning is limited to select groups within the company. The process does not include consumers as institutional participants. In government, on the other hand, even planning documents must be open to the public because of the Freedom of Information Act. In a private company, strategic planning documents are usually confidential because of concern that information will leak to competitors.

Planning for major policy issues of government often involves interagency coordination and rivalries. For example, the government's efforts to improve employment opportunities for low-income persons must relate to problems under the responsibility of agencies other than the Department of Labor such as: day care, health, vocational training, drug abuse programs, economic development, tax incentives, or others. Coordination of planning with other agencies and obtaining their support is sometimes difficult because of natural bureaucratic tendencies to be concerned primarily about areas for which they are directly accountable.

SEPARATION OF POWERS AND CHECKS AND BALANCES

An important conceptual difference between government and private industry is the separation of powers and the principle of checks and balances which provides the backdrop for the structure and responsibilities of our government.

The United States Constitution grants all legislative powers to Congress. This wide range of powers includes providing ". . . for the common defense and general welfare of the United States . . ." and setting and collecting taxes. The executive power is vested in the President. The President's power to make treaties and to appoint many of the top officials in departments and agencies is conditioned on his receiving the "Advice and Consent" of the Senate.

The President recommends to Congress ". . . such Measures as he shall judge necessary and expedient . . ." but they are not implemented unless enacted by Congress. After enactment, Congress has a further check on the President's power, because Presidential budget requests must be approved by Congress through the appropriations process. In addition, there is continuous Congressional oversight of Executive Branch administration.

The Constitution provides a check on the power of Congress and the President by vesting judicial power in the Supreme Court and other federal courts. Judicial power extends to several categories of cases including those arising under the Constitution and the laws enacted by Congress.

In practice, the Constitution created a system of separate institutions sharing power. The checks and balances, such as Presidential veto, Congressional oversight, Senate confirmation, and judicial review, ensure that power is shared. In recent years, for example, the Executive Branch has devoted greater efforts to preparing elaborate and carefully documented legislative proposals and then attempting to guide them through the legislative process. At the same time, Congress has become more involved in the administration of programs in areas such as staffing levels, organizational structure, and in some cases, reserving the authority to approve or veto regulations issued by an administrative agency with authority to implement a statute.

The careful balancing of powers between the branches of government reflects our unwillingness to give complete authority for government policy to one person or group of persons or to a single institution. This blurring of responsibility, this ambiguity of power, is the basic principle of our political system, but it is also the antithesis of one of the basic principles of management — to establish a center of authority with provision for accountability.

The head of a government bureau has more limited authority than his counterpart in private industry. In private industry, a Chief Executive Officer typically has the authority to make budget decisions except for major capital expenditures which require approval by the Board of Directors. In contrast, the head of a government bureau cannot set the level of his bureau's budget; instead, it must be submitted to the department head for review. The department head then submits a departmental budget request for review to the Office of Management and Budget, which serves as budget officer for the President. The President then submits his budget to Congress as a request for appropriations. It must be approved by the Senate and the House and signed into law by the President. The OMB then apportions the funds to the department which allocates them to the bureau head.

The time lags inherent in the governmental budget process illustrate the way the separation of powers and the resulting bargaining process affect the time frame for budget planning. The head of a large government agency usually starts work within his agency on its budget proposal at least six months before transmittal to the President. After reviewing and modifying agency proposals, the President submits his proposal to Congress about four months later, which is also nine months before the fiscal year begins. Congress may take the entire nine months to act on the President's request. In fact, in recent years, Congress has often appropriated funds after the fiscal year has started. In other words, an agency head starts working in about March 1978 on his budget for the fiscal year beginning in October 1979. In private industry, the entire budget planning process from initiation to final approval to start of the fiscal year rarely takes more than nine months.

Heads of government agencies do not have full power to hire and fire employees. Instead, they must obtain approval to hire from the Civil Service Commission, a separate federal agency. Dismissals can be appealed to the Commission and often delay the process substantially. Even reorganization plans must be approved by the Civil Service Commission or, in some cases, by Congress. The salary structure established by statute and its accompanying regulations severely restrict an agency head's flexibility to use compensation for rewarding employees.

Separation of powers is particularly relevant in considering strategic planning in the context of government. Plans formulated by agency heads become recommendations to the President and eventually, in some cases, to Congress. Strategic planning focuses extensively on goals and objectives, but Congress has authority to establish agencies and their purposes, define organizational location, programs, staffing, funding authorization and appropriation levels, and exercise oversight functions regarding all agency activities. Obviously, Congress plays a central strategic planning role in government.

LACK OF PROFIT MOTIVE

The primary goal of a business firm is to earn a profit. If the firm does not earn profits, at some point it will cease operations. Similarly, if one of its products does not earn a profit, at some point the firm will stop manufacturing and/or selling that product. The results of the firm's overall activities and any individual product can be quantified, measured over time, and compared with competitors and alternative investment opportunities.

The profit motive or "bottom line" provides a discipline to business firms that is different conceptually from goals and performance measures in government. Government does not have an overriding, single-purpose goal similar to "profits." As quoted earlier, Congress is to provide ". . . for the common defense and general welfare of the United States . . ." and the President is to recommend ". . . such Measures as he shall judge necessary and expedient . . ." These are very general purposes that often require Congress and the President to balance conflicting interests. When considering whether a program should be enacted, government policy makers often must decide which groups in our society should benefit and which groups should bear the cost. Many government policy issues relate to questions of redistributing income, problems that cannot be "solved" scientifically because they involve a person's basic view of society and a series of value judgments. Aside from these policy goals, of course, each agency usually has a common goal of survival and growth.

In government there is no quantitative "bottom line" like profits that is a common measure of performance and a basis of comparison accepted by all constituents. It is extremely difficult, if not impossible, to terminate a government program. Each government program has a group of persons or a constituency that benefits from the program. With many programs, the constituents form a lobbying organization to represent their interests and present their views to Congress and to the Executive Branch. Let's assume that a group of 10,000 constituents is benefiting, or will potentially benefit, from a $50 million grant program. The potential benefit to them is about $5,000 per constituent which compares with the average cost per person in the United States of about $0.25. Obviously, the added cost to the individual taxpayer is so low that he has very little interest in devoting his time to lobbying against the program. Generally, those lobbying on an individual program are greatly biased in favor of continuing the program, and the government official has no quantitative measure to help him assess the statements made by the constituents.

Fundamentally, programs are evaluated through elections, Congressional oversight, Presidential direction, by interest groups, political parties, and press scrutiny. In addition, certain techniques, such as program evaluation, have been developed to measure the performance of government programs. Program evaluation is a technique that looks at the objectives of a government program, reviews its impact, and determines whether there are more efficient ways of accomplishing the same objectives. Evaluating government programs often includes the use of control groups and cost/benefit analysis in an attempt to quantify, to the greatest extent possible, the impact of a program. These tools are helpful, but there are serious methodological disagreements among experts on proper techniques, and they are generally considered to be at an early stage of development. There is also a problem of deciding how to group government programs together for evaluation purposes and, of course, serious resistance to evaluating sensitive programs.

PERIODIC LEADERSHIP TURNOVER

Periodic elections are an integral part of our political system. Executive Branch leadership positions are related to the electoral process which has an important impact upon management and planning in government agencies. Whenever a new president is elected, he usually appoints an entirely new slate of heads of agencies and subcabinet officials. In addition, his appointees have authority to select over 2,000 persons for noncareer positions, many of which are high level. The potential exists for a completely new top management team in executive branch agencies every four years.

Between elections, turnover among political appointees serving in agencies is very rapid. Assistant Secretaries average less than two years in their jobs. During the eight years of the Nixon-Ford presidency, there were four Secretaries of Health, Education and Welfare, four Secretaries of Commerce, and five Secretaries of Labor. This type of change in leadership and executive turnover differs from management changes in private industry. Managers in private firms have a longer term attachment to the firm, and although they may only serve in a particular job for a short period of time, they provide continuity to the overall management policies.

When changes in top management positions occur, private firms usually attempt to show how the change will provide continuity to the firm's leadership in a systematic, planned manner. It is a common practice for the CEO to "groom" his successor by moving him into Chief Operating Officer or Vice Chairman positions for one or two years prior to assuming leadership.

Political terms of office and frequent turnover between elections require that strategic planning in government be geared to a four-year cycle. An agency head is bound to meet difficult obstacles or knowing acquiescence from his staff if he attempts to plan strategically for a period when his staff members know that he will no longer be there, and that most likely there will be major shifts in policy by the newcomer. Operational planning in this context is more successful because it usually focuses on decisions that are less sensitive to the personal wishes of the agency head.

The short-term nature of high level government policy positions also discourages long-term planning. A policy official has little incentive to spend his time on problems that will not occur until after his term of office or on new initiatives for which his successor will receive credit.

Periodic elections and frequent turnover provide an environment that accentuates political skill and visibility rather than administrative skills. The political process places a high premium on the ability to handle effectively a wide variety of short-term crises. A call from a Congressman about a problem faced by an influential constituent, a White House meeting to help formulate policy options for the President, a luncheon speech, and testifying before a Congressional committee all in one day is not an unusual schedule for an agency head. In this highly charged, fast moving environment, there is rarely little incentive for good management, and policy officials frequently place a low priority on managing well the programs already enacted.

A NOTE ON DEFINITIONS

As discussed earlier, considerable confusion exists over the use of the term "planning." The following paragraphs describe other government activities that are sometimes referred to as "planning" but do not fit the working definition of planning set forth in this study. In some cases, they are related to elements of planning.

Program Evaluation. Program evaluation is an attempt to assess the impact of a program after it has been operating. It often includes an attempt to measure the extent to which program participants or the economy benefit, along with the incidence of the costs incurred. It sometimes includes an analysis of whether there are more effective ways of accomplishing the same objective. Given current methodologies, quantifying the impact of a program is extremely difficult; the results are often subject to varying interpretations. Evaluation studies are extensive for some programs, such as manpower training, head start, efforts to rehabilitate ex-offenders, air quality regulations, and various education programs.

Forecasting. Government agencies currently devote considerable effort to forecasting or determining in advance various important events or trends. These forecasts are educated guesses, since no one knows for certain what will happen in the future. The methodologies vary, sometimes utilizing surveys, straight-line extrapolation of trends, or econometric models that take into account the past relationship of variables believed to be important. Examples of widely used forecasts include forecasts of demographic trends, industry trends, and capital expenditures by the Census Bureau, forecasts of the labor force and occupational trends by the Bureau of Labor Statistics, and forecasts of the gross national product, inflation rates, and other economic variables by the Council of Economic Advisers, the Office of Management and Budget, and the Treasury Department.

Bottleneck Analysis. When there is concern about a current or potential future shortage in an industry or sector of the economy, government agencies are sometimes called upon to do analyses of bottlenecks which could be caused by a sudden surge in demand for a particular product or by a sudden reduction in the supply of raw materials that are used to produce a product. Bottleneck analyses are often initiated because of concern that the price of a raw material or a series of products has increased or will increase in the future. These microeconomic analyses usually include an investigation of the change in underlying supply or demand conditions, a forecast of future conditions, and in some cases, if warranted by the analysis, recommendations for government action to alleviate the problem.

Bottleneck analyses are often done by *ad hoc* task forces appointed specifically for that purpose. The Council on Wage and Price Stability has statutory responsibility to perform such analyses for individual industries or sectors on an ongoing basis. Examples of bottleneck analyses conducted by the Council on Wage and Price Stability include coal and cement. *Ad hoc* task forces have conducted such analyses for the construction industry and various building materials, especially lumber.

Macro-economic Goal Setting. The Employment Act of 1946 declares the objective of federal economic policy: "to promote maximum employment, production, and purchasing power." Economic programs and policies are to be consistent with "other essential considerations of national policy," and all are to be carried out by means "calculated to foster and promote free competitive enterprise and the general welfare . . ." The Act requires the President to transmit an economic report each year that sets forth such matters as current and foreseeable trends in employment, production, and purchasing power, and it outlines a program for carrying out the policy declared in the Act. In some cases, presidents have set specific numerical goals for macro-economic indicators such as unemployment rates or inflation.

Detailed Government Resource Allocation. With this kind of national planning or national economic planning, the federal government would make decisions on how resources are to be allocated, what goods and services are to be produced, and how they are to be distributed. Production targets would be set on an industry-by-industry basis, and the government would then attempt to influence allocation of raw materials, capital, and human resources to make sure that the targets are met. This kind of planning does not exist in the United States today, although in certain highly regulated industries, such as airlines, trucking, and railroads, the government sets prices, controls entry of producers, and determines whether service can be introduced or curtailed. During World War II, our country came closest to national economic planning on an economy-wide scale.

4

FINDINGS AND CONCLUSIONS

WHAT IS PLANNING?

It is unfortunate that the findings and conclusions of a study must start with a section defining the subject of the study, but that is a commentary on the misunderstandings and confusion so common in this field. If a person is asked "Do you favor planning?" his first response should be "What do you mean by planning?" because the questioner can have completely different definitions of planning in mind.

Planning is defined broadly as ". . . a process of deciding what to do and how to do it before some action is required." This definition is sufficiently broad to include planning by an individual, corporation, or government agency.

For purposes of this report, planning is defined as a process that includes:

1. Setting goals or objectives

2. Assessing and forecasting factors in the external environment (e.g., economic growth, inflation rates, changes in public attitudes, and actions of foreign governments)

3. Designing and assessing alternative courses of action to achieve the goals

4. Selecting the best course of action

5. Evaluating results as the course of action is implemented

The first element, setting goals or objectives, and the last, evaluation, are the two key elements that distinguish planning from other types of forward thinking. If goals are established, together with a feedback mechanism that measures progress and continually modifies courses of action to accomplish those goals, planning becomes a process of managing as opposed to merely thinking in advance about future problems.

LACK OF A CORPORATE PLANNING MODEL

The central concern of this study has been to appraise corporate planning experience and to determine what lessons, if any, government can learn from that experience in seeking to improve its own planning activities. The study was directed at the need for mechanisms of strategic and operational planning as conducted at the federal level. Specifically excluded was the kind of "national planning" or "national economic planning" that involves detailed government resource allocation.

No single corporate planning model is commonly accepted in major companies in the United States. Instead, corporate planning varies widely among companies depending on the industry, mix of products, degree of decentralization, organizational structure, and management style of the Chief Executive Officer and other top management officials. There are common patterns in some of the activities (e.g., forecasting) included in the definition of "planning" used in this study, but in general, planning systems are tailored to the unique characteristics of the organization and the top management.

A number of research studies, often using different definitions, have attempted to assess the impact of corporate planning. Although many companies use corporate planning extensively, few of these studies found evidence that corporate planning is associated with successful business operations or higher profits. This does not mean, of course, that planning is not associated with higher profits, only that these research studies have not found conclusive evidence to that effect.

LACK OF TRANSFERABILITY TO GOVERNMENT

Planning needs between business and government differ because of intrinsic differences in functions, responsibilities, and purposes. Even if there were a common model or apparatus for corporate planning in private industry, its transferability would be limited, and it would require substantial modification to make it suitable for use on a widespread basis in government. In our democratic society, planning by government takes place within a political environment. Congress, the Executive Branch, and the courts are all institutional participants in policy making, and it is a bargaining process. Interest groups, political parties, and the media also exert influence in policy making.*

A fundamental difference with private industry is the separation of powers among the branches of government and the principle of checks and balances. Government agencies are not able to act as independently or with the same degree of autonomy as a private company.

Government does not have an overriding and narrowly focused single-purpose goal similar to profits. Instead, government has broader goals such as providing ". . . for the common Defense and general Welfare of the United States . . ." Government has no quantitative "bottom line," like profits, that is a common measure of performance and a basis of comparison accepted by all constituents. In private industry, the results of a firm's activities and any individual product can be quantified, measured over time, and compared with competitors and alternative investment opportunities.

---

*Memorandum of comment by JAMES Q. WILSON: While the author of this paper is properly cautious about the ease of implanting strategic planning methods in federal government agencies, I believe that the incautious reader is likely to draw the unwarranted conclusion that a factual case has been made for the benefits such methods are likely to produce or that the barriers to the adoption of these techniques can be overcome. My reading of the Constitution and of American political history makes me skeptical that anything even faintly resembling the corporate planning model can or should be adopted by government agencies or Congress.

Periodic elections result in frequent changes in Executive Branch leadership positions. Managers in private industry have a longer term attachment to the firm, and although they may serve in a particular job for only a short period of time, they provide continuity to the overall management policies. The short tenure in high level government policy positions also discourages long-term planning.

IMPORTANCE OF PLANNING IN GOVERNMENT

Strategic planning, operational planning, and program evaluation are important activities that have the potential for improving the performance of government agencies and should therefore be encouraged. Better planning will lead to more rational analysis, but it may not necessarily lead to more rational decision making and better government policies. Policy decisions in government are made in the context of the political process which sometimes precludes rationality. Nor will better planning automatically solve many of our social problems, such as the poverty cycle or urban blight. Our knowledge of cause/effect relationships and what works and what doesn't work is just not that sophisticated. For now, the assumption that better formal planning will result in better government policies should be accepted on faith as is the assumption that better corporate planning results in improved profits. However, this is an area that deserves analysis and investigation.

Encouraging increased planning and evaluation in government is a difficult task. The political environment of government discourages long-range analysis in part because the pay-off often comes at a time when the initiator does not get the credit. The media, interest groups, and political parties must apply political pressure on Congress and the President to provide the impetus for this kind of activity.

One of the central themes of this study is that there is no panacea or major solution in private industry that can be transferred to government to solve its diverse planning needs. Instead of further attempts to identify approaches to planning that can be transferred from business to government, it appears more profitable to analyze the agency problems that need improved planning and to identify approaches to planning to meet these needs. With this in mind, some general principles derived from corporate and government experience can be useful.

SETTING GOALS AND PERFORMANCE OBJECTIVES

Within a democratic political context, the elected representatives of the people should be held accountable for setting public policy goals. Clearer goals would undoubtedly result in improved efficiency in government programs. When goals are clear, measurement and control are facilitated, and decentralization of planning and implementation becomes possible.

In practice, the political process of policy making usually requires compromise. Consequently, the end product is imprecise and goals are often poorly defined. In some cases, goals are purposely kept vague because Congress or the Executive Branch cannot agree on the goals for a program or agency. The agency head then must attempt to select his own program goals through a bargaining process with the other participants. The vagueness of the goals makes it difficult for Congress or the President to hold an agency head accountable for performance since it is unclear what the standard should be.

Statutory goals also sometimes conflict. The Environmental Protection Agency (EPA), for example, attempts to preserve the environment conflict directly with Department of Energy (DOE) efforts to increase production of oil, coal, and natural gas, and to conserve energy. Reducing auto emissions increases gasoline consumption. Adding safety equipment to automobiles increases costs while increasing gasoline consumption because automobiles are heavier.

Because broad policy goals are often the result of a bargaining process, Congress and the President should attempt to establish short-term performance objectives for a program as clearly as possible. They should also create an evaluation mechanism that would make the agency management accountable. Instead of becoming involved in the minutiae of administrative agency decisions, elected officials should set clearer goals and performance objectives and hold agencies accountable. To be successful, planning systems must attempt to improve the efficiency of government, but at the same time, they must adapt to political realities.

Short-term objectives for a government program should not be considered sacrosanct and should be modified over time as external events change, societal values change, and more experience is gained with the program. Unfortunately, from the standpoint of the politician, changing publicly stated targets is difficult because it appears to be a sign of failure. Nevertheless, if more specific goals are to be meaningful, they must be changed periodically or they will lose their relevance and become a facade for the true progress of the program.

ROLE OF PROGRAM EVALUATION

Program evaluation, which is an attempt to assess the impact of a program after it has been operating, should become an integral part of planning and management in government. In some cases, machinery and organizations to perform program evaluations already exist; in others new mechanisms must be established. Profits and losses provide some general evaluation of the success or failure of products in private industry. Program evaluation attempts to provide some of the same information regarding a government program to policy makers and their constituents. Given current methodologies, quantifying the impact of a program is extremely difficult, and the results are often subject to varying interpretations. The results of program evaluations must be reviewed critically and they should not be used as the only input in deciding whether to terminate a program. Nevertheless, program evaluations can produce some helpful inputs to policy makers, and they should be encouraged.

Program managers should not be asked to evaluate the impact of their own programs. Aside from the potential conflict of interest, they are not usually equipped methodologically to conduct such studies. An independent office reporting directly to the department head should be given this responsibility. Several cabinet agencies such as HEW, HUD and Labor have already adopted this organizational format. Program managers should devote their efforts to other types of evaluation studies that primarily focus on improving the efficiency of existing programs.

DIVERSE PLANNING SYSTEMS

The size and diversity of the federal government preclude the solving of all of its planning needs by any single planning system for every agency. Agency functions differ greatly, and agency approaches to planning must be designed to meet the specific needs of each agency. The Office of Management and Budget could perform a valuable function if it required each agency to develop its own planning mechanism, prescribed some general standards for agency planning systems, and served as a clearinghouse for information on agency systems. Efforts by OMB to mandate a single uniform planning system for all agencies would be counterproductive unless it allowed each agency to take into account its unique function.

In designing these systems, however, it must be kept in mind that many of the policy problems faced by an agency cross departmental lines. Helping low-income persons or families become self-sufficient, for example, may require changes in welfare policies (HEW), housing policies (HUD), manpower training policies (Labor), drug abuse policies (Justice), and economic development policies (Commerce). Furthermore, issues change over time, and organizational structures cannot anticipate or reflect each of these changes. For such planning issues, mechanisms must be developed for interagency participation. Ideally, this cooperation should take place before an agency submits a recommendation for a new policy or program to the President or the Office of Management and Budget. Developing this type of participation in government is often difficult, however, because of the lack of clearly defined goals and the constituency-oriented nature of many agencies.

INVOLVEMENT OF TOP MANAGEMENT

Top management must be involved for any planning process to work effectively. As with any management function, leadership by example is essential. This involvement is especially important for strategic planning because the Chief Executive Officer in a private firm often brings a unique focus to bear and is able to decide questions relating to the basic issues addressed in strategic planning. The CEO because of his position has a unique overview of the company, including its strengths and weaknesses. He can assess the capability of his top managers better than any other single individual. His vision of the future prospects for the firm's products or product lines is an especially important input into the planning process if it is to be useful. Finally, his managerial judgment in balancing economic, technological, and human factors determines whether the company will be successful.

In government, the principle of top management involvement must be modified to meet the unique environment. The purposes of an agency are included in its legislative mandate, and Executive Branch directives, as well as court decisions, and many major strategic decisions require legislation. The agency head still plays an important strategic policy role, but his authority is much more limited than his counterpart in private industry. Many more persons and groups participate in the policy-making process than would do so in private industry. Strategic planning becomes a process for the agency head to formulate a recommended course of action to higher authorities, executive and legislative.

PLANNING AND IMPLEMENTATION

Planning cannot be conducted successfully by support staff without the serious involvement of operating levels. Planning and implementation responsibilities should not be divided. When they are separated and something goes wrong, the implementor blames the plan and the planner blames the implementor. Private companies and government agencies who have turned over the responsibility for planning to a department or group of staff persons without insisting on the active involvement of operating divisions find that elaborate, fancy, but unrealistic plans result. Of course, an important distinction exists between involving operating divisions and uncritically accepting all of their recommendations. Operating divisions usually tend to focus on short-term problems and do not have the same company-wide or government agency-wide overview as a CEO or a staff group whose responsibility cuts across the entire organization. At the same time, however, they are much more familiar than staff planners with the specifics of their industry and the operating problems of implementing new policies. Their cooperation and assistance is crucial to the success of many new ventures. For these reasons, the perspective of both operating and staff personnel is crucial.

In government, career employees have much more longevity than agency heads and their top staff. If career employees do not view the plan as realistic, it can be vitiated over time. This underscores the importance of involving career employees in the planning process.

THOROUGH ENVIRONMENTAL UNDERSTANDING

The necessity for developing a thorough understanding of the environment in which an organization operates was discussed earlier. Many private firms have developed sophisticated market research capabilities to study constantly consumer needs and reactions to their products. They have also become increasingly knowledgeable about their sources of raw materials and potential future bottlenecks. This type of environmental research and understanding has become even more important as firms encounter more rapid environmental and structural change.

As private firms and government agencies become larger, it becomes increasingly difficult for company and agency leaders to maintain contact with their customers and clientele. Providing up-to-date information to the decision maker is a critical principle of good planning.

In government it is essential for policy makers to have accurate information about the problems they are attempting to address. Because there is no market place test for most government services, it is important to assess constantly the extent and changing nature of the problem. For example, statistics on the poverty population and their income do not always include in-kind transfer payments. Unemployment statistics do not always provide an accurate understanding of the extent of hardship experienced by certain groups.

Developing improved statistics and data bases is a long-term effort in government. The federal government's present statistics-gathering efforts take place in several different statistics-gathering agencies. In recent years, however, some effort has been made to avoid overlap and to prevent gaps in statistics through the efforts of the Office of Management and Budget.

A CONTINUING DIALOGUE

The above general principles were derived from both corporate and government experience. Given the diversity of government agencies, these principles must be utilized within the context of the specific agency problems that need improved planning. In this connection, a series of in-depth discussions between government and industry planners and users of planning would be beneficial. Both the project advisory committee and the government officials who participated in our discussions found it very useful to have such dialogue.

APPENDIX

EXAMPLES OF CORPORATE AND GOVERNMENT PLANNING SYSTEMS

This appendix includes seven case studies describing planning processes in four private firms and three government bureaus. Each firm prepared a description of its planning process. The government bureau studies were prepared from agency handbooks and other written descriptions of bureau planning processes and from interviews with bureau policy and planning officials. The case studies were reviewed by the bureaus for factual accuracy. The studies were not based on observation by the author of the actual process of planning. It is important to emphasize that these case studies describe the formal process of planning. Planning practices may actually vary from the formal process depending on personalities, management style, unforeseen events, and other factors.

GENERAL ELECTRIC COMPANY

General Electric Company is a highly diversified multibillion dollar a year manufacturing company. At General Electric, strategic planning is a pervasive management discipline as a result of:

1. Many years of management and employee training in business analysis methods
2. A special accent on the "strategic" dimension required in business planning
3. The design, implementation and experience with six cycles of its annual strategic planning process from 1971 to 1976
4. The development of approximately 200 highly qualified and trained full-time strategic planning staff

5.   Sustained top management involvement in, and support of, the importance of strategic planning in enhancing company performance

General Electric's strategic planning had its roots in a basic company tradition and style — one of strong training in analytic managerial methods.

Strategic planning at General Electric aims to help management:

1.   Be alert to a multitude of environmental changes affecting its wide diversity of businesses; in particular, identify the effectiveness of its business approaches in contrast to the many competitors of General Electric (General Electric competes with over eighty of the top two hundred U.S. industrial corporations)

2.   Identify, develop, and allocate resources in support of business strategies, including managerial, people, financial, technical, and production resources

3.   Identify broad problems and opportunities facing many businesses of the company in order to define corporate objectives, strategic thrusts, and to improve the total business environment

4.   Be a management system that helps lead, motivate, and control the diverse and complex worldwide activities of the company in the interest of shareowners

Thus, strategic planning in General Electric is particularly designed to help manage the company's broad range of businesses.

THE PLANNING PROCESS

General Electric's diverse products and services, serving many industry sectors, are organized into forty-four Strategic Business Units (SBUs). As part of the annual planning process, each SBU develops a comprehensive strategic business plan, or updates it, each year. SBUs are defined therefore as the point in the organization where all business functions, resources, and environmental perspectives can come together to develop an effective strategic plan, usually against an identifiable external competitor. The process follows the following major steps:

1. January - February: Review of environmental trends to pinpoint problems, opportunities, and strategic issues. Corporate and SBU level issues are combined in planning guidelines for the year.
2. February - June: SBU General Managers, together with their planning and functional staffs, formulate or update the business' strategic plan.
3. June - August: Each business strategic plan involving significant change is reviewed for validity, consistency and effectiveness in coping with environmental conditions.
4. September: The priorities for resource allocation are reviewed at the corporate level and consideration given to alternate objectives or strategies. Guidelines on short-term operating goals are set.
5. October - November: SBUs prepare their operating plans and detailed budgets.
6. December: Final budget reviews are made and the total corporate budget tested for consistency with overall strategic priorities.

This planning process is "standard" and is based on the concept of deciding longer-range strategy first, then fitting short-range operating goals into the longer-term plan. The distinctive feature in General Electric's case is that the system handles forty-four SBUs. To accomplish this in sufficient depth, selectivity is required in each cycle, that is, certain businesses are given more or less attention each year. The strategies of most businesses need to be reviewed in depth only every two or three years.

The decentralization of this planning process ensures that, while objectives are approved centrally, the creative task of strategy development to meet objectives is carried out decentrally, where most product and market knowledge exists. The system, therefore, retains control of company direction while harnessing decentralized knowledge and creativity.

General Electric develops a corporate plan which attempts to "add value" and to complement the decentralized planning of its individual businesses. The corporate plan needs to be more than a documentary summation of forty-four individual business plans. The corporate plan complements SBU strategy development by providing an actionable base-line for identifying, distinguishing, and resolving corporate level strategic issues.

MANAGERIAL SUPPORT FOR PLANNING

Supportive motivation and leadership is critical to the success of a decentralized planning system. Ideas will fall on stony ground if the wrong environment exists. For example, if the managerial environment places too great a stress on near-term financial results, managers will over-emphasize short-term performance at the expense of the longer-term development of the assets entrusted to them.

Performance screens are used to balance the emphasis on short-term and longer-term performance when awarding compensation increases and bonuses. Performance factors include managerial actions that would benefit the business in the future, for example, product development, market diversification, facilities improvement, people, and strategy development. Annual achievement goals in each of these areas are agreed upon at the beginning of the year and reviewed at year-end. In the growth businesses, future benefit performance factors carry more weight in determining a manager's bonus than short-range financial results. Conversely, in harvest situations, strong emphasis remains on short-term financial results. Thus, managers with different strategic assignments can achieve high rewards.

Another feature of leadership and motivation has been the willingness of management to maintain its strategic priorities through the recession-inflation conditions of 1974 and 1975. Severe cost reductions had to be made, but they still reflected strategic priorities. Additionally, support for new products and ventures was discussed and maintained even at the toughest times.

THE IBM CORPORATION

The IBM Corporation develops, manufactures and services a wide variety of information-handling products. Most of these products fall into the broad areas of data processing, office products, advanced technology development, and special information systems for federal government use. IBM is a multibillion dollar company that receives about one-half of its revenues from outside the United States.

ORGANIZATIONAL PHILOSOPHY

Insofar as planning is concerned, IBM's philosophy of organization is implemented as follows:

1. IBM activities are grouped into a number of operating units which, where feasible, have profit/loss responsibility. These units are differentiated by business area and geographic region and have the range of functions needed to conduct their assigned missions as autonomously as practical.

2. Operating unit management is responsible for development and implementation of its plans. Prior to implementation, plans are reviewed and approved by corporate management. Performance against plan is measured and controlled by operating unit management and monitored by the corporate staff. Periodically, the results of operations are also reviewed and approved by corporate management.

3. Business policies are controlled at the corporate level and provide the broad framework within which all operating units function.

4. In its review and assessment of the operating units' plans and performance, corporate management is assisted by the corporate staff, which provides counsel and performs certain centralized services

THE PLANNING PROCESS

Operating unit management maintains an awareness of emerging problems or opportunities which may affect its business. Concurrently, within their respective areas of functional expertise, the various corporate staffs are also monitoring change. When an event or trend of potential significance is detected (e.g., slackening of economic conditions in a country they serve), the operating unit affected will alert corporate management as to the magnitude and timing of the expected effects. In some cases, the unit is joined by the corporate staff in developing and recommending a course of action. Once accepted, these recommendations are then built into the unit's plan by its management. Where a problem is of major and continuing importance (e.g., energy), a joint council involving affected units and staffs will be created to monitor and recommend action on a regular basis.

The planning and control system pervades the entire structure of the organization. It serves as a primary communication link between corporate and operating unit management for establishing unit objectives and strategic direction, negotiating plan commitments, and measuring performance against plan. The bulk of the planning done within IBM is not only decentralized into the several operating units, but within any given unit, planning is further decentralized to the plant and laboratory levels.

As indicated at the outset, planning and implementation are line management responsibilities. However, planning staffs to support line management exist at the corporate, operating unit (and where these are large, at the divisional or country) and plant/laboratory levels. The size and mix of these staffs depend on the specific responsibilities of the line managers they support. At the operating unit level, the executive will normally have finance and planning, as well as the functional skills needed to develop a properly balanced profit plan. For example, his staff will review and assist in integrating the various product plans into the unit plan. The unit executive makes the final judgments as to business volumes to be achieved, resources required, and risks to be accepted.

At the corporate level, the line executives also have finance, planning, and other functional staffs to assist them. For example, among the responsibilities of the Corporate Business Plans staff are design of the company planning system, establishing plan guidance and data requirements, managing the plan schedule, recommending profit targets for the various operating units, and reviewing and assessing their strategies and plans.

There are two distinct but interactive kinds of planning within the IBM system — Program Planning and Period Planning:

1. Program planning (e.g., a program to develop a product or improve the productivity of a function) is characterized by the following: The program plan generally has a single objective, but may involve several functional elements. Its time horizon is determined by the nature of the specific program objective and the work processes required to achieve it, its cycle for review and decision making, and by the inherent dynamics of the program. At any point in time, each operating unit has a large portfolio of product and functional programs in various stages of planning and implementation

2. Period planning complements program planning and is characterized by the following: The period plans balance among multiple program and other objectives to achieve the profit targets assigned. Its time horizons are fixed by Corporate management, being two years for the operating plan and five years for the strategic plan. The cycle for review and decision making is tied to the calendar to ensure the availability of an operating budget for each unit at the beginning of each year

PERIOD PLANNING

In its overall planning system, each IBM operating unit annually performs both strategic and operating planning. The purpose of strategic planning by a unit is to establish its business direction; that of operating planning, to implement the direction within budgeting requirements and commit the unit to achieving planned results.

STRATEGIC PLANNING

The strategic planning process is as follows:

Corporate Targets and Operating Unit Goals

Corporate management assigns targets (profit and profit margin) to each operating unit. In response, each operating unit management develops and assigns goals to its product/system and to functional management to guide their strategy development.

Strategies

Operating units with development responsibilities prepare and maintain product/system strategies to serve as the foundation for their marketplace offerings. All units prepare functional strategies to ensure that the most effective organization and business approaches are used to achieve increasing productivity of resources. As part of its marketing strategy, a unit may assign industry goals and develop strategies to meet the needs unique to specific customer sets.

Strategic Plan

The strategic plan integrates the several product/system and functional strategies of the unit, presents the financial results over the plan period, and compares planned results against corporate targets. This plan (and selected strategies) is submitted to the Corporate Management Committee (CMC) by the operating unit executive. The plans are reviewed by the corporate staff, and prior to CMC review, their assessments are forwarded to the CMC and the operating unit. Among the bases for these assessments are:

— Consistency with approved strategic direction
— Balance between objectives sought and resources required
— Relationships to plans of other operating units
— Excellence in each functional area

Certain staffs also write short critiques as to the strengths, weaknesses, or risks associated with the individual plans. On the basis of these staff inputs and the operating unit presentation, the CMC approves the units' proposed business direction, resolves nonconcurrences, reevaluates its targets, and reassigns them.

To support this planning work, the operating units with product development responsibility generate product assumptions; Corporate Economics provides the economic and environmental assumptions; and the various corporate staffs issue functional guidance as necessary. Other factors and trends are monitored and analyzed to determine their possible implications (e.g., environmental issues, consumerism, privacy and data security, and international political and economic relationships).

Using the product and economic assumptions, the forecasting department of each operating unit produces an overall set of business volumes by integrating the individual product forecasts, previously developed, with the results of the supply-demand balancing against the order backlog. These volumes provide management with a projection based on explicitly defined and quantifiable factors. Management then applies judgment to take into consideration the unquantifiable considerations previously mentioned, and the adjusted business volumes are distributed to the various functions as the basis for their plans. Based on historical experience, each function then uses its own planning factors and models to translate these volumes into workload, resources, and cost/expense. Computer models are widely used at both the operating unit and Corporate levels. For example, all manufacturing activities use computers extensively for balancing supply against demand and determining plant loadings; engineering uses them for design automation; marketing and service for territory analysis and proposal preparation. The unit staff then integrates the several functional inputs into a properly balanced plan; the unit executive approves and submits it to corporate management.

As one approach for dealing with the problems of uncertainty, corporate management may request contingency analyses to test, for example, the effect of a more extreme set of economic assumptions on unit plans. Corporate Economics will then issue two outlooks, one for the base plan, and a second for the contingency plan. Operating units will then develop two plans and review them with corporate management. This approach has proven useful in improving the speed and flexibility of response to unanticipated conditions.

OPERATING PLAN

Based on the business direction in the approved strategic plan and including changes as necessary, the unit then develops an operating plan that focuses on implementation over the year plus two. This plan contains detailed business volumes and workload forecasts, and functional resources and financial plan commitments. These data are developed through planning processes similar to those for the strategic plan described above. The operating plan is used to establish budgets and other objectives for the next year. Certain units provide selected revenue and resource items in a long-range outlook at the time of the plan submission to show the probable extended effects, risks, and exposures of the proposed plan. After approval by the operating unit executive, the plan is submitted for corporate review and assessment (as it is for the strategic plan). The CMC resolves nonconcurrences and approves the unit plan.

When significant deviations occur in actual results versus plan, a unit may request approval for changes in its operating plan. All requests are coordinated by the Director of Budgets (and, indeed, may be initiated by him); those requiring CMC approval are reviewed and assessed by appropriate corporate staffs.

FORD MOTOR COMPANY

The Ford Motor Company is a multibillion dollar automotive manufacturing firm with several associated businesses.

The process of long-range planning at Ford involves three steps:

1. Setting enterprise objectives or goals
2. Establishing policies, procedures, and assumptions necessary for carrying out long-range planning
3. Developing specific strategies to achieve the company's goals

A corollary aspect of planning is the maintenance of a reporting system through which actual or projected-actual results are compared with the plans on a recurring basis.

THE PLANNING PROCESS

Ford has had no formal "planning office" that has as its sole and complete duty the development and administration of long-range plans. As an evolutionary step, however, Ford is in the process of establishing an organization to integrate strategic and business plans and to extend its planning horizons; accordingly, the planning process described herein is historic in nature. The central staffs play the major role in the development of goals for the company and its various components. The staffs also review specific plans developed by the operating activities and maintain a set of reports designed to measure progress toward objectives. The basic formulation of forward plans, however, remains the responsibility of the operating divisions (or, in certain cases, of specified staff activities that work in areas beyond the scope of any division).

Ford Motor Company has selected two principal goals:

1. To increase substantially (by a designated amount) its profits per share in the next few years
2. To reach an objective (and specified) rate of return on assets

Ford admits the validity of many supporting objectives — social responsibility, acceptable governmental relationships, strong market share, first-class product quality, customer loyalty, research capability, physical growth, management development, public image, investment stability — but it seems clear that all these are contingent upon solvency and profit-making potential. A central frame of reference based on profits (whether in terms of absolute dollars, return on assets, return on sales, or some other variation) seems the most practical and effective basis for corporate long-range planning. From this goal important subsidiary plans, ranging from expanding political participation by employees to stimulating authorship of original scientific theses, can be developed.

After the corporate goals are established, it is necessary to set up subgoals for the specific operations. The profits-per-share goal has not been "farmed out" to each division, partly because one of its chief virtues — easy identification with the interests of stockholders as represented by directors — may be less effective in a component that does not actually face the discipline of annually confronting its own stockholders. Segments of the profit-per-share goal have, however, been assigned to broad groups of activities.

The second goal, rate of return on assets is established for each of Ford's divisions and subsidiaries. These are termed "profit centers." The meaning of this term, to Ford, is that the manager has responsibility for most of the variables associated with the operation of his business. There are, of course, limits on these responsibilities; most of their United States divisional managers, for example, operate under a company-wide labor agreement in which they have relatively little voice. Similarly, buyer-seller relationships are inevitably less autonomous among some of their divisions than among outside firms.

Ford's *detailed* plans generally extend only four or five years into the future. They have found that it is unnecessary in their industry to require the development by operating divisions of detailed plans for the longer range. On the other hand, broader strategic plans have a longer time horizon. The gestation period of most planning is three to four years. Each division is assigned a rate-of-return goal that it is expected to reach, under reasonable projections, within three to four years. Of course, the company's long-term objective may exceed the sum of these shorter-range divisional goals, and this leads to the establishment of specialized groups whose missions are to explore the longer-range implications of changes in technology, national and international economic growth, and basic research directed toward the long-range development of entirely new product lines. They do not, however, find it wise or necessary to spell out the missions of these groups in specific, year-by-year financial commitments. When such programs become reasonably well defined, they are assigned to one or more operating divisions, where a specific manager may be held accountable for making financial commitments for a given time period and for submitting detailed plans to achieve the commitments.

The goals — corporate profits per share and corporate and divisional returns on assets employed — are reviewed annually under the direction of the Office of the Chief Executive; they are changed if and when changes seem warranted. For example, during a period of rapid decline in the value of the dollar, it is necessary to raise the earnings-per-share goal in order to maintain the real earning power of the enterprise. Similarly, fundamental changes in predicted growth rates for various elements of the business might dictate reductions in some divisional profit objectives and increases in others. An annual review of the goals in these terms appears practical and effective.

The company's top management continues to stress the importance of long-range planning throughout the organization. To many, the necessity of planning seems obvious. Long-range business planning, however, is relatively new, and they find it necessary to remind their people periodically of its importance. Long-range planning has top-management acceptance at Ford. One objective is to broaden this acceptance to include all levels of management.

This effort takes many forms, such as temporary task forces devoted to strengthening the planning process in areas where it has been weak, and compensation of personnel based in part upon performance in doing the planning job. The purpose is to emphasize that planning is everyone's business and that it is a never-ending business.

Several basic assumptions must be set forth before long-range planning can be done intelligently. These assumptions, drawn up by various staff groups, include predictions of price levels, government fiscal policies, population trends, productivity rates, and similar factors. These assumptions, and any changes in them, are communicated to divisional planners, who are not expected to duplicate the work of the staffs in these areas.

STRATEGIES TO MEET
THE COMPANY'S OBJECTIVES

Ford Motor Company develops several separate sets of Plans: The Product Plan, the Divisional Plan, the Research Plan, and the Supplementary Plans.

The Product Plan

In this industry, planning the product — its package size, functional characteristics, styling, investment, piece cost — is central to success.

As an essential supplement to product planning, Ford has a product profit reporting system, designed to summarize the financial consequences of a company's future plans. The purpose of this forecasting system is to provide top management with a balanced, coordinated, and clearly understood picture of the company's future profits. It forecasts profits for the company as a whole and for each major product line, based on present plans. It is neither optimistic nor pessimistic; its task is to give the best possible prediction of actual results.

The system provides recurring reports of company-wide profits by product line and by division for the current year and four future years, compared with several prior years as a frame of reference. Each report stresses the actual and projected rate of return on assets and enables top management to appraise the degree of progress toward the company's objective.

The Divisional Plan

Another framework in planning is based on divisions, rather than on product lines. As mentioned earlier, each of Ford's divisions is a profit center and a responsibility center. Therefore, the company has set up a planning and control system based on divisions. This is coordinated through Ford's profit plan and budget system and is supervised by Finance Staff.

Their Plans are prepared for five future years. The budget

for the next year is prepared in detail; plans for the succeeding four years are prepared in more general outline form. It is here that their long-range plans are blended into short-range operating strategies.

The task of preparing profit budgets is the division's. Actually, preparation starts at the plant level and then moves to the division general office level. The Finance Staff's functions in the profit-budgeting process are to provide uniform standards for budget preparation, to review each budget for reasonableness, and to see that a proper task has been set for the division. Frequently, this involves considerable discussion with the division; it remains the division's job, nonetheless, to prepare the budget. Next, the division has the job of preparing plans that will enable it to attain its objective rate of return on assets within the planning period.

It is clear that divisionally oriented budgets can bring concentrated attention to areas of profit improvement that are not likely to be highlighted in the product plan. For example, these include control of administrative costs, improved control of scrap, more efficient freight patterns and shipping methods, and better use of data-processing equipment. Top management finds the two planning systems to be complementary and mutually reinforcing, despite some inevitable degree of overlap.

The Research Plan

The long-range future of the company also requires coordinated planning of a different nature — less explicit, broader-ranging, and oriented toward fundamentals instead of toward specifics. These studies comprise a "Research Plan," with the term used to include not only scientific and technical research, but long-range economic and market analyses. At Ford they have not yet brought the "Research Plan" to a stage where it attempts to project, year by year and in profit and loss terms, the results of the planned research. Rather, it is a systematic statement of *who* has been assigned to study *what*, *when* they will issue reports, and *what decisions must be made* with regard to the reports. Without such a coordinated plan, it is impossible for top management to find out what each of the groups is studying, much less to determine how their studies should be synthesized, and which should be pursued most aggressively.

The Supplementary Plans

The comprehensive profit and research plans are supplemented by specific planning aimed at certain variables, primarily nonfinancial in nature, that are essential to attaining Ford's long-range objectives. These variables are of sufficient importance to justify specific planning, even though they might be covered to a reasonable degree as subcomponents of the other plans. Examples are management development, product quality, and supplies.

Ford has set objectives and developed specific strategies to attain their goals. Responsibility for these key variables has been set; progress is measured and reported to top management.

Several additional points about the planning process should be made here. First, the various planning frameworks do not always mesh together neatly; in fact, they occasionally clash head on. Sometimes this indicates that planning is not as good as it should be. At other times it reflects separate approaches to a common problem. In these instances, Ford thinks the cost of duplication is more than offset by the advantages of different approaches. Second, the "how" of their planning frequently changes, reflecting altered planning needs. Finally — a point that may be obvious — the most sophisticated planning and reporting system cannot ensure success. Brilliant styling, creative engineering, efficiency in production, and in cash management cannot be *guaranteed* by the development of a strong planning process. Planning must be kept in perspective, as a set of tools to help good men do their best and to spot weaknesses early. It cannot be considered as a substitute for direct managerial effort. There are people who have the ability to prepare and present glowing plans but who lack the personal drive necessary to carry out the plans. Again, the presence of a comprehensive, management-oriented reporting system helps minimize the adverse effects of such overplanning. The "paper tigers" are likely to curb their enthusiasm a bit if they realize that the control system will inevitably track actual accomplishments and measure them against the plans.

MANUFACTURERS HANOVER TRUST COMPANY

Manufacturers Hanover Trust Company is a large multibillion dollar bank holding company consisting of several affiliated banks and bank-related subsidiaries.

The corporation benefits from its formal planning process in the following ways:

1. Coordination among various divisions is improved because planning helps ensure that all appropriate business information is passed from one area of the corporation to another.
2. Senior management is alerted to plans and strategies at all levels of the organization. This results in better decisions and a firmer sense of purpose and direction. Although active decisions on major issues command close senior management attention, the planning process helps ensure that management is equally aware of a decision to take no action on a particular problem or opportunity.
3. Employees' motivation is improved since managers know what is expected of them, and there is wide participation in the planning process at various management levels.
4. There is a positive attitude toward change within the organization as a result of its involvement in the planning process.

PHILOSOPHY OF PLANNING

In 1971, Manufacturers Hanover Trust Company established a Corporate Planning Department to assist in the development of formal divisional and departmental plans throughout the organization.

Implicit in the planning process is the principle that managers must be concerned continually with the long-term implications and results of decisions. Therefore, members of the senior officer team in each unit participate personally in the creation of the unit's plans and in the implementation of its programs. Manufacturers Hanover believes that management's commitment to planning is the most important component in the planning process.

Within Manufacturers Hanover Trust Company, each division, department, subsidiary, and affiliate has a designated corporate planning coordinator whose role is to organize the unit's plans. He develops, with senior management, overall divisional goals and strategies for the Five-Year Strategic Plan. This entails guiding units within the division in such matters as new products and services, monitoring specific projects, and providing management with progress reports on implementation of strategies. In addition, the planning coordinator is responsible for ensuring that the division's Profit Plan (a one-year plan similar to a budget) is consistent with the Strategic Plan, that the Profit Plan meets corporate guidelines, and that all variances of actual results from Plan are reported to management and their consequences considered.

THE PLANNING PROCESS

Manufacturers Hanover Trust Company's planning process includes two interrelated phases: The Five-Year Strategic Plan and the One-Year Profit Plan which includes a Major Expenditure Management System and Quarterly Management Reviews.

The purpose of the Five-Year Strategic Plan is twofold: (1) To develop the primary documents which identify the components of the near- and long-term earnings flows, and to help ensure that these flows are at optimal levels; and (2) in the written support documents, its purpose is to develop awareness of the internal and external factors influencing the future of the corporation.

Each unit focuses on the various aspects of its business and its overall direction, assesses its business environment, and analyzes its strengths, weaknesses, and alternatives. Each unit states its objectives and goals, followed by strategies and alternative strategies designed to realize these long-term objectives. After this process is completed, an abbreviated financial statement is prepared on a divisional and, subsequently, on a corporate basis. In June of each year, all units in the corporation present to senior management their Strategic Plans for the five-year period beginning the following January.

By contrast, the One-Year Profit Plan has a higher level of detail and greater tactical commitment. This plan is usually presented to senior management in December, immediately preceding the beginning of the Profit Plan year. It includes detailed proposals for revenues and expense as well as sources and uses of funds. The more tactical aspects of the plan outline specific programs to be implemented by the business unit during the year, in line with the strategies presented in its Five-Year Plan.

From the Profit Plan, variance analyses against actual performance are developed to track progress and to make appropriate operating changes. Following each of the first three quarters of the year, each unit prepares a written analysis of the major variances between actual and planned results. These analyses are then presented to senior management at Quarterly Management Review meetings. Variances from the Plan for the entire year, based on preliminary financial information, are reviewed each December when the following year's Profit Plan is presented to senior management.

In order to provide senior management with an overview of the funding required and corporate tax impact of each unit's major projects (over $100,000), Manufacturers Hanover employs a Major Expenditure Management System. This management system includes gathering financial data pertaining to major projects, the application of various financial measurement techniques to determine the return on incremental investment, and the tracking of actual expenditures from budget. If a major project is anticipated, each unit is required to submit a Major Expenditure Estimate report to senior management at the annual Profit Plan review.

At the conclusion of the Strategic Plan and Profit Plan cycles, the financial numbers are consolidated. Manufacturers Hanover then uses computer models to assess various alternative courses of action and alternative interest rate and loan demand scenarios. The impact of these scenarios is assessed for tax planning, capital planning, and other corporate purposes.

THE PLANNING PROCESS IN THE NATIONAL BUREAU OF STANDARDS

The National Bureau of Standards was established in 1901 to provide a national system for physical measurement and to provide various services to improve the use of materials and the application of technology. Today the NBS is one of the nation's largest physical science research organizations, with a full-time staff of 1,600 professional and 1,450 non-professional employees. The Bureau's budget for fiscal 1977 is $123 million; direct Congressional appropriations account for about 55 percent of NBS funds, with an additional 39 percent resulting from work performed by NBS for other government agencies such as the Department of Housing and Urban Development, the Department of Energy, the General Services Administration, and the Food and Drug Administration. The sale of NBS goods and services, such as calibrations and standard reference materials, provide the final six percent of the NBS budget.

Located within the Department of Commerce, the National Bureau of Standards is headed by a Director and is organized into four major institutes:

1. The Institute for Basic Standards provides the central base within the United States for a complete and consistent system of physical measurements and coordinates that system with measurement systems of other nations. It furnishes the research and essential services leading to accurate and uniform physical measurement and reliable data in science, industry, and commerce.

2. The Institute for Materials Research conducts research concerning the basic properties of matter and materials and develops standards for measuring such properties. The Institute also develops, produces, and distributes standard reference materials which provide the bases for calibration of instruments and equipment, facilitate comparison of measurements on materials, and aid in the control of production processes in industry.

3. The Institute for Applied Technology is concerned with the development and application of science and technology in such areas as building performance, fire safety, consumer product performance and safety, energy conservation, and electronics. This institute is also responsible for the voluntary product standards and national voluntary laboratory accreditation programs, for assisting in maintaining uniform weights and measures regulations and procedures in the 50 states, and for providing a library of national and international standards.

4. The Institute for Computer Sciences and Technology develops standards and provides scientific and technical guidance for the effective use of computer and automation technology in the federal government.

The other major operating unit within NBS is the Experimental Technology Incentives Program. ETIP investigates the effectiveness of various incentives and mechanisms to stimulate increased development and use of technology by industry. All Bureau operating units are supported by central offices for administration, program development, and information services.

STRATEGIC PLANNING

Long-range strategic planning at the National Bureau of Standards is a highly structured, analytic process focused on the development of agency goals and program priorities. The planning process also provides an opportunity for developing and expanding constituency support and for achieving coordination both within the agency and with other institutional participants in the policy process. Responsibility for long-range planning is centered in an Executive Board comprised of the Director of NBS and his deputy, the associate directors for programs, administration and information, and the four Institute directors. The planning process includes a Long-Range Planning Conference, an Executive Board Strategy Conference, and a Strategy Feedback Conference. All planning activities are coordinated by the Program Office.

The NBS Long-Range Strategic Planning Process

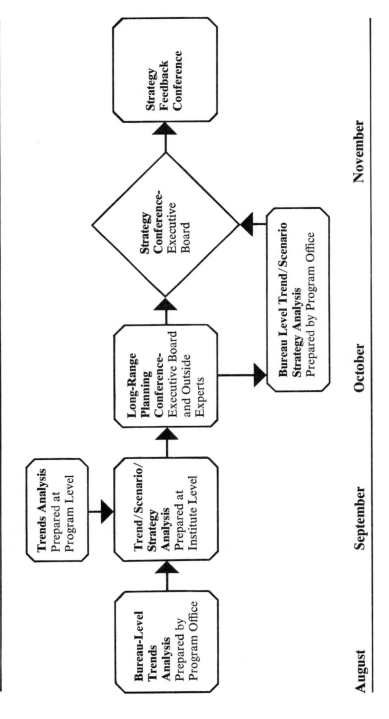

August   September   October   November

LONG-RANGE
PLANNING CONFERENCE

Long-range planning is initiated with preparation of a forecast of trends by the Program Office to appraise operating units of anticipated conditions in the external environment over a six-year period. This analysis examines:

1. Trends in White House, OMB, and departmental policies concerning research and development; the identification of trends in NBS relationships with other federal agencies, including the mix of civilian and defense funding, size of contracts, types of services; and emerging needs of state and local governments which might be met by NBS

2. Trends in Congress relevant to NBS, such as probable future effects of new Congressional mechanisms (e.g., the Office of Technology Assessment and the Congressional Budget Office; implications of increased scientific and technical staffing in committees and in the Congressional Research Service, general perceptions and trends in Congress concerning science and technology policies; and the federal role in research and development)

3. Identification of long-term economic trends, including budget and employment policies, and the impact of economic factors on science and technology

4. Trends in the industrial community which will require NBS support and which will affect the Bureau's functions, including assessment of trends in industrial research and development, identification of emerging technologies, identification of industrial trends for use and interaction with the voluntary standards system, and industrial perceptions of trends in federal science and technology policies

5. Trends in the scientific community relevant to NBS, such as trends in university science and other scientific institutions, the availability of scientifically trained personnel, and so forth

6. Trends in major national issues, such as long-term trends in the resolution of the energy crisis (e.g., probable federal energy policies, trends in energy research and de-

velopment funding, anticipated needs for measurements and standards, and probable effects of energy shortages on research and development for other technologies)

On the basis of the Program Office forecast and projections of scientific and technological trends developed by operating units at the program and bench level, each Institute prepares detailed "Trend-Scenario-Strategy" analyses of major issues bearing on their programs. Such analyses identify significant future trends; evaluate the consequences of these trends in terms of Institute programs, organization, resources, and status as scientific research centers; and outline alternative program objectives and strategies for Executive Board consideration at a Long-Range Planning Conference.

The Long-Range Planning Conference is an attempt to develop a Bureau-wide perspective of the external environment over a six-year period in order to facilitate the setting of priorities, selection of program objectives, and the anticipation of technical, managerial, and administrative requirements. At the Planning Conference, the Executive Board critically evaluates the analyses of long-term trends and possible strategies developed by the Institutes and hears presentations by outside experts on such topics as "Implications for Science and Technology of Emerging National Policy Issues," "Problems and Directions in the Federal-Industrial Research and Development Partnership," "OMB Criteria for the Federal Role in Research and Development," and "Future Needs for Measurements Standards."

EXECUTIVE BOARD STRATEGY CONFERENCE

The Program Office prepares a summary-critique of the Long-Range Planning Conference, and this then serves as the basis for an Executive Board Strategy Conference where final debate and decision on Bureau objectives and strategies takes place. During the Strategy Conference, important trends and issues are reevaluated in the context of the Bureau's legislative mission and the anticipated budgetary climate. Current organizational goals and responsibilities are also examined. The

Executive Board then makes judgments concerning future
goals, program priorities, and the most appropriate organizational strategies to pursue.

STRATEGY FEEDBACK CONFERENCE

The long-range planning process culminates in a Strategy
Feedback Conference during which the Director and other
members of the Executive Board outline Bureau goals, program objectives, and strategies to technical division chiefs and
program managers.

Following the Strategy Feedback Conference, the Executive Board monitors implementation of its decisions during the
program and budget preparation cycles and during program
execution.

PROGRAM AND PLANNING REVIEWS

The long-range planning process is supplemented by an
extensive series of program and planning reviews. Four principal review mechanisms are utilized:

1. NBS internal management and planning reviews
2. NBS contracts with the National Academy of Sciences to
    provide an independent, external review and evaluation
    of NBS programs
3. Special evaluations of selected program or issue areas by
    contractor personnel "under the direct program manage-
    ment of the NBS staff"
4. A statutory visiting committee of five members which re-
    ports annually to the Secretary of Commerce on the
    efficiency of NBS scientific work and the condition of its
    equipment

INTERNAL REVIEWS

Internal management and planning reviews are conducted
at each level in the organization. These reviews culminate in

an extensive series of program presentations made by the program managers to the Director and the Executive Board. The reviews are structured to assess the technical performance of each program and to assess the relevance of each program to Bureau mission and to long-range plans. (Approximately 10-15 percent of the Bureau programs are "turned over" each year during the review process and their resources reallocated.) The review process provides NBS management with an analytical basis for determining program priorities and a means to identify program changes and improvements which can be effected by management action. It also provides a mechanism for surfacing policy and program problems for management consideration. In addition, such reviews serve as a means to reassess and sharpen goals and strategies developed during the long-range planning process.

EXTERNAL REVIEWS

To obtain an external perspective, NBS contracts with the National Academy of Sciences to provide an independent review and evaluation of NBS programs. The 29 NAS panels, which evaluate individual Bureau programs, are comprised of approximately 250 top-ranking scientists and engineers selected by the National Academy of Sciences from industry (50 percent), universities (40 percent), and government (10 percent). The panels work closely with program managers and the principal staff of each program in examining technical performance, the relevance of program objectives, and areas for future program change and improvements. The NAS panels report their findings and recommendations to the program managers and to the Director of NBS. In addition, the chairman of each NAS evaluation panel reports to the Statutory Visiting Committee, and panel findings are published by the National Academy of Sciences. Conducted on an annual basis, panel evaluations are particularly helpful in relating Bureau programs to constituency needs and for "improving the effectiveness with which program outputs are delivered."

The Organic Act of 1901 created a Statutory Visiting Committee of five members which reports annually to the

Secretary of Commerce on the efficiency of NBS scientific work and the condition of its equipment. The entire Bureau is surveyed and evaluated by the Statutory Visiting Committee. Long-range goals and strategic plans are a central focus of this review. Examples of the types of long-range planning concerns raised by the Visiting Committee with NBS management are listed below:

— "If you look at NBS and picture what it's going to look like over the next five or ten years, what do you see? What would you like NBS to look like?"

— "What is your total budget now and what are the Institute budgets? What will the budget picture look like in five years? What would you like it to look like?"

— "Visualize getting a Secretary of Commerce who really understands the Government's role in technology and wants to expand NBS as an economic contribution to the country. How would NBS respond to this?"

The evaluation conducted by the Statutory Visiting Committee thus provides another mechanism to assess, modify, and formulate long-range Bureau goals and strategic plans.

OPERATIONAL PLANNING

NBS line managers and project leaders are responsible for developing plans for implementing Bureau-level goals formulated during the long-range planning process. Such "bottom-up" operational planning is closely linked with program budgeting and is executed through a modified MBO (Management by Objectives) process. The main instruments for operational planning include the "NBS-228 Project Report" prepared by project leaders and the "Subcategory Document" prepared by Institute directors. These documents provide a mechanism for integrating and refining the goals of managers and operating personnel at each level of the organization and a means for tracking progress toward goal attainment. The "NBS-228 Project Report," for example, is an operational plan for current year work which includes MBO objectives, milestones and completion dates, and a report on progress made during the previous year. The "Project Report" represents "both a contract and agreement of understanding" between the project leader, associated investigators, section and division chiefs, and the program manager. The "Subcategory Document" serves as a report from Institute directors to the Director of NBS. It contains a first draft of the next year's budget document and a presentation of MBO objectives and milestones, and it details operational goals and alternative strategies for achieving them.

Both the NBS-228 Project Reports and the Subcategory Documents are periodically reviewed, at various levels of the Bureau and departmental hierarchies, to measure progress and evaluate accomplishments. More importantly, perhaps, the MBO objectives, justifications, milestones, and other information developed during such operational planning provide an important analytic base for subsequent long-range planning efforts. A reciprocal relationship thus exists between operational and strategic planning at NBS.

THE PLANNING PROCESS IN THE FEDERAL BUREAU OF PRISONS

The Federal Bureau of Prisons is responsible for the care and custody of persons convicted of federal crimes and sentenced by the courts to serve a period of time incarcerated in a federal penal institution. The Bureau carries out this responsibility.by operating a nationwide system of 49 maximum, medium, and minimum security prisons, halfway houses and community program offices. Individuals confined to such institutions are provided a variety of services, including counseling, work training, education and recreation. The federal government currently spends about $275 million per year for the care and custody of 32,000 imprisoned offenders. The annual cost per offender averages $8,400.

Overall supervision and coordination of Bureau of Prisons operations is provided by a central office in Washington.

The Washington office issues standards and policy guidelines and retains responsibility for those activities not directly delegated to regional or field management levels. Regional offices are responsible for the management of Bureau institutions and programs within specific geographic areas.

NEEDS ASSESSMENTS

Planning activities at the Bureau of Prisons focus on the construction and operation of prison facilities. The Bureau's planning process is initiated each year with the issuance of long-range (two to three years) planning guidelines by the Washington office to regional and field installations. At the field level, resource needs are identified and then submitted to the regional office where such facilities and staffing requirements are analyzed within a regional context. Each region then establishes priorities for institutional needs and submits to headquarters only those needs that can be realized "within a predetermined budgetary increase constraint." The predetermined increase constraint is placed on institutional and regional managers "to assist them in identifying only their highest priority needs."

TEN-YEAR PLAN

In conjunction with the process of needs assessment, regional and Washington office staff participate in the development of a ten-year plan to identify goals and alternative strategies for meeting long-range facilities requirements. This entails an analysis of the existing prison population and projected changes in the long-term population, the formulation of objectives concerning basic quality standards for future prison facilities, and the development of capital investment alternatives, including consideration of new facilities and the mix of conventional incarceration vis-a-vis community-based programs.

The Bureau of Prisons has no control over the number of inmates and types of offenders in its custody, their length of stay (commitment) or the geographic distribution of its clientele. In practice, the courts and U. S. attorneys determine the number of prisoners entering custody of the Bureau, and the Parole Board determines the number of prisoners leaving.

The socioeconomic factors and the operations of the Federal criminal justice system which affect prison population are constantly changing. For purposes of planning, however, it is necessary to develop an estimate of what the population will be ten years in the future. Therefore, historical prison population data is analyzed concerning the average age, sentence, time served, and the recidivism rate of offenders, and these factors are correlated with data concerning race, sex, educational level, type of offense, and geographic distribution. The Bureau utilizes the national unemployment rate as an important indicator for projection purposes. The size of the young adult population is another important factor. Because the size of the future prison population may also be influenced by changes at various points in the criminal justice process, possible revisions of the Federal Criminal Code, trends concerning levels of enforcement, number of U. S. attorneys, prosecution rates, conviction rates, and sentencing and parole policies are also monitored.

Once an estimate of the anticipated federal prison population is arrived at, facilities requirements are identified and long-range objectives formulated regarding such factors as the size and types of future institutions, location, the amount of living space to be accorded inmates and the mix of conventional incarceration with community-based programs and other correction methods. These long-range objectives serve as the basis for the development of alternative capital investment strategies for federal prison construction. An effort is made to coordinate strategy development with planning activities in the Criminal Division of the Justice Department, the U. S. Attorney's Office, the Board of Parole, and corrections agencies at the state and local levels.

PLANNING DECISIONS

The alternative strategies formulated during the ten-year planning process and the needs assessments developed by the regional offices are evaluated, in terms of cost estimates and manpower requirements, etc., by an Executive Staff Budget Review Committee. The Committee makes recommendations as to program priorities and identifies areas for increase in congressional appropriations requests. The Director of the Bureau of Prisons together with an Executive Staff Committee make final judgments regarding long-range goals and program priorities, including the construction of new facilities. All subsequent administrative actions concerning management of the Bureau of Prisons are directed toward implementing these decisions.

THE PLANNING PROCESS IN THE NATIONAL PARK SERVICE

The National Park Service was established in the Department of Interior in 1916 to administer national parks and national monuments for the enjoyment of the public and to protect and conserve the national environment, historic objects, and wildlife in these areas. Today the park system consists of 293 areas and 20 affiliated areas (including national parks, national monuments, national recreation areas, and other types of areas) ranging in size from a tenth of an acre lot to parcels of millions of acres that sometimes transcend state boundaries. New statutes are periodically enacted to set aside additional land for inclusion in the park system. The Park Service's budget for fiscal year 1977 is $492 million. The Park Service is headed by a Director and is administered through nine regional offices. The service has a staff of 8,943 full-time and 4,978 seasonal personnel.

In the National Park Service a major planning effort is focused on determining the future use and management of geographic areas that have been set aside as units of the national park system. The objectives of this decentralized planning activity are to identify problems and define park management goals, to design and assess strategies for achieving such goals, and to provide an analytic basis for agency decision making. Secondary objectives of the planning process include developing and expanding constituency support for the operating programs of the Park Service and achieving coordination both within the agency and with other institutional participants in the policy process. The planning process in the Park Service involves the following steps:

1. The development of management objectives designed to achieve a park's purpose
2. The identification of planning tasks required to achieve the objectives
3. The specification of a method for conducting the planning tasks
4. The collection of sufficient information to place the park in a regional context and to permit the formulation and analysis of alternative strategies for meeting management objectives
5. The development of alternative strategies and the analysis of their probable consequences
6. The selection of the most acceptable strategy; the documentation of the rationale for its selection; and the evaluation of the nature, significance, and controversiality of its consequences; and the formulation of a general management plan and environmental impact statement, if appropriate
7. The elaboration of proposals included in the selected strategy and the further assessment of consequences

MANAGEMENT OBJECTIVES

Initial Park Service planning efforts are directed towards preparation of a management statement which identifies the park's purpose, analyzes various factors that influence or constrain park management, reviews existing land use classification within the park, and develops management objectives for achieving a park's purpose. Each park must have an approved statement for management, which is subject to annual review and revision by the regional and Washington offices.

A park's purpose is usually defined by (or deduced from) enabling legislation or other legal documents providing for the park's creation (e.g., memoranda of agreements, presidential proclamations, secretarial guidelines, reports from Congressional hearings, or the Organic Act of the Park Service). Because many units of the national park system were authorized decades ago when different environmental and social conditions prevailed, park purpose is carefully reexamined during the preparation of management statements, and if necessary, corrective legislation to redefine park purpose is proposed.*

The management statement also includes an analysis of the legislative and administrative constraints on management and use of the park, and it identifies regional and other factors which may influence park management (e.g., specific environmental problems, activities or organizations outside the park's boundaries that affect and/or are affected by the park, etc.).

The development of management objectives for such functions as cultural resource management, natural resource preservation, visitor protection and safety, and visitor information, is the central purpose of the management statement. Management objectives provide a framework for conserving park resources, for integrating the park into a regional environment, and for "accommodating environmentally compatible public use" in accordance with existing Park Service policies. All subsequent administrative decisions concerning the management, use, and development of the park are directed toward achieving these objectives and fulfilling the park's purpose. In essence, the management objectives are a list of desired conditions.

Preparation of the management statement is scheduled by the regional office and is undertaken by the park superintendent with policy guidance and technical assistance from the regional and other office staffs. At various stages during preparation, and when a draft statement is completed, public review is solicited.

---

*No planning activities are undertaken for areas not presently within the park system. Instead, "new area studies" are undertaken for land proposed for inclusion in the park system to determine significance (in terms of natural resources), to determine feasibility (boundary determination problems), and to evaluate management alternatives both within and outside the park system.

PLANNING REQUIREMENTS

After management objectives have been defined, planning requirements and schedules to achieve a park's management objectives are identified by the park superintendent with assistance from the regional office and a central planning staff located in Denver. An outline of planning requirements usually contains a statement of the problem or situation for which planning is required, a list of the planning tasks and information needed to resolve the problem or improve the situation, identification of those responsible for accomplishing the planning tasks, cost estimates for the tasks involved, and a list of all plans currently in effect. The outline of planning requirements is reviewed and modified by the regional office and, along with the region's proposed planning program, is submitted to the Washington office where national planning priorities are established. Such planning requirements are reviewed and updated annually.

INFORMATION BASE

Systematic park planning requires gathering information concerning ecological and cultural resources of the park and its region, information on the physical facilities of the park and the capability of such facilities to support existing and projected uses, data concerning visitor characteristics and their influence on park use, and the data concerning various socioeconomic factors. Such information provides the basis for the formulation, analysis and comparison of alternative planning strategies, and for specific decisions on the management, use, and development of the park within a regional context.

ALTERNATIVE STRATEGIES

Through the design and analysis of alternative strategies, Park Service planning seeks to ensure that all reasonable ways of achieving management objectives have been considered and that both the beneficial and adverse consequences of implementing each strategy have been identified. Such a process may also result in the identification of conditions or problems that necessitate changes in management objectives.

Included in this phase of the planning process are the following activities:

1. Analysis of management objectives to ensure that they are not outdated and are still valid; new objectives are also formulated and evaluated if necessary
2. Development of feasible alternative strategies for meeting the objectives
3. Identification and quantification of the effects of alternative strategies on the natural and cultural resources of the park and its region
4. Analysis of the socioeconomic implications of each strategy for the park
5. Analysis of the effects of each strategy on visitors and on the kinds and amounts of public use of the park
6. Analysis of the effects of each strategy on park management
7. Estimates of the costs, manpower requirements, and time frames of each strategy

The analysis of strategies is reviewed by the regional office to evaluate the relative importance of technical, monetary, managerial, and other factors, and to make a determination as to the significance of the environmental consequences of the various alternative strategies.

GENERAL MANAGEMENT PLANS

Upon completion of the strategy review by the regional office, a park-wide general management plan is prepared by an interdisciplinary planning team for use as a management tool and as a public statement of management intentions.* This plan charts a long-range strategy for resource management, visitor use, and park development at a level of detail to facili-

---

*The planning team includes the park superintendent, other park personnel, and specialists from the central planning staff in Denver. Private citizens with specialized knowledge of the park may also be members of the planning team.

tate implementation of proposed actions. The general management plan also specifies requirements to ensure compliance with relevant legislation and administrative policies and procedures.

The general management plan is the central planning document for units of the National Park system. It defines long-term management objectives for a park and provides a strategy to achieve them. The general management plan is used by the park superintendent as well as by the regional and Washington offices. Preparation of a general management plan is a major undertaking, requiring two to three years to complete at a cost ranging from $200,000 to $1 million. Because of the time and financial costs involved in the planning process, priority is given to the preparation of complete general management plans for recently authorized parks, parks without approved plans, and parks where existing plans are outdated. For parks with adequate general management plans, planning requirements are generally limited to implementation plans.

Every general management plan contains:

1. A statement of the park's purpose and management objectives
2. Proposed management zoning for all lands and waters within parks
3. Interrelated proposals for resource management, visitor use, interpreting park resources, and general development

Other elements to be contained in or added to the plan, as needed or applicable, include, but are not limited to:

1. A land suitability analysis to determine factors limiting types and amounts of acceptable uses
2. A determination of legislation needed for boundary adjustments and other purposes in order to meet management objectives
3. Detailed development strategies, prepared to define specific proposals for substantial development in new or existing areas
4. Detailed resources management strategies, prepared to specify needed research and provide comprehensive direction for resources management activities
5. Detailed strategies for interpretation

6. Wilderness reviews, prepared to determine the suitability of lands within the park for designation as legislative wilderness under provisions of the Wilderness Act

The component parts of the general management plan are periodically reevaluated and revised to reflect changes in management objectives or in ecological, social, or economic conditions.

The general management plan (or its independently prepared components) is subject to policy review in the Washington Office prior to approval by the regional director.

In larger parks, implementation plans dealing with specific sites or subjects may be required to supplement the park-wide general management plan. Such additional plans, upon completion and approval, become part of the general management plan. (In smaller parks, the general management plan may be sufficiently detailed to eliminate the need for implementation plans.) Implementation plans generally focus on such activities as management of one or more wildlife species and vegetation within the park's ecosystem, management of natural and prescribed fires, backcountry use and its regulation, concession needs, and contracted visitor services.

COMPLIANCE REQUIREMENTS

Park Service planning must comply with a wide variety of legislative and executive requirements. All planning efforts, for example, must be consistent with the requirements of Section 106 of the National Historic Preservation Act of 1966 and a 1971 Executive Order dealing with "Protection and Enhancement of the Cultural Environment." In addition, the Park Service planning process must comply with the provisions of the National Environmental Policy Act of 1969. NEPA compliance requires:

1. A systematic, interdisciplinary approach to planning, and objective consideration of environmental values

2. Full involvement of other agencies and the public during the planning process

3. Procurement and use of relevant environmental information in analyzing alternative strategies
4. Recordkeeping on planning activities as a basis for decision making and preparation of documents
5. Preparation of an environmental statement when the plan as a whole constitutes a major federal action or entails significant or controversial impacts

Among the other laws and administrative orders that are relevant to Park Service planning are the following:

Acts of Congress
The National Park Service Organic Act of 1916, as amended
The Wilderness Act of 1964, as amended
The Department of Transportation Act of 1966, as amended
The Airport and Airway Development Act of 1970
The Fish and Wildlife Conservation Act of 1934, as amended
The Endangered Species Act of 1973
The Marine Protection, Research, and Sanctuaries Act of 1972
The Federal Water Pollution Control Act, as amended
Safe Drinking Water Act
The Wild and Scenic Rivers Act, as amended
The Water Resources Planning Act of 1965
The Coastal Zone Management Act of 1972
The Land and Water Conservation Fund Act of 1965, as amended
The Clean Air Act, as amended
The Noise Control Act of 1972
National Trails System Act
The Uniform Relocation Assistance and Real Property Acquisition Policies Act of 1970
Concessions Policy Act of 1965
Freedom of Information Act

Executive Orders
Executive Order 11295, "Evaluation of Flood Hazard in Locating Federally Owned or Financed Building, Roads, and Other Facilities, and in Disposing of Federal Lands and Properties"
Executive Order 11752, "Prevention, Control, and Abatement of Environmental Pollution at Federal Facilities"

Administrative Orders
Department and National Park Service directives

Office of Management and Budget directives (e.g., OMB Circular)

COORDINATED PLANNING EFFORTS

The plans of outside agencies and interests affect and are affected by proposed actions within units of the National Park System. Coordinated planning, therefore, is needed to integrate the park into a regional environment and to ensure that potential conflicts are minimized.

Joint agency planning is usually undertaken when a park is adjoined by Indian reservations, other federal lands, state lands, or lands subject to state, regional, or local planning or regulation. Formal agreements are made to coordinate major Park Service planning efforts with other planning agencies and governmental bodies.

Joint and coordinated planning efforts are undertaken for such problems as the provision of facilities and services for visitors within and outside the park, zoning and other land use controls for lands in the park's vicinity, and management planning or regulation of facilities or activities by other government agencies which affect the park's environment (e.g., reservoirs, highways, flood control projects or pollution control).

PUBLIC PARTICIPATION IN PLANNING

Park Service policy and various laws provide for public participation at various stages of the planning process. The Park Service thus takes positive actions to involve the public as early as possible in the planning process, before planning decisions have been made. Workshops and meetings are held to inform the public that a plan is being prepared, to solicit information, and to bring to light public concerns, particularly with regard to controversial issues. Once the planning process is underway, informal workshops are held with the planning team and members of the public to acquire information on technical aspects of the plan and matters of existing or potential conflict. Formal meetings are held to provide the public with an opportunity to evaluate various alternatives under consideration, and to comment on the content of the analysis. Finally, draft plans are available for public review for a period of at least 30 days prior to an administrative decision.

REQUIRED CONSULTATIONS

In addition to cooperative planning activities and public participation, certain consultations with other parties are required by law. Many parks, for example, have legislatively established advisory boards, and regional advisory commissions have been established by the Secretary of Interior. In addition, the National Environmental Policy Act of 1969 requires consultation with any other federal agency which has jurisdiction by law or special expertise with respect to a plan's environmental impacts. Other laws, such as the National Historic Preservation Act of 1966, require that specified agencies be given an opportunity to review and comment on Park Service plans affecting historic resources before a planning decision can be approved.

ABOUT THE AUTHOR

Michael H. Moskow joined Esmark, Inc. in July 1977 and was elected Vice President (Corporate Development and Planning) in February 1978. His responsibilities include coordination of Esmark's planning system, review of capital expenditure requests, and mergers and acquisitions.

Mr. Moskow began his government service in August 1969 as a Senior Staff Economist with the Council of Economic Advisers and subsequently served in six additional government positions including: Under Secretary of Labor, U. S. Department of Labor; Director of the Council on Wage and Price Stability; Assistant Secretary of Policy Development and Research, U. S. Department of Housing and Urban Development; Assistant Secretary for Policy, Evaluation and Research, U. S. Department of Labor; and Executive Director of the Construction Industry Collective Bargaining Commission.

In 1978, Mr. Moskow was nominated by President Carter and confirmed by the Senate to be a member of the National Commission on Employment and Unemployment Statistics. In April 1978, he participated in the U.S./U.S.S.R. Seminar on Management Decision Making in the Soviet Union under the joint sponsorship of the Soviet State Committee for Science and Technology (GKNT) and the Center for International Management Studies.

Prior to government service, Mr. Moskow taught economics and was Director of the Bureau of Economic and Business Research at Temple University. He also taught economics at Lafayette College and Drexel University. He is the author of four books and over 20 articles in professional journals.

Mr. Moskow holds an A.B. in Economics from Lafayette College, and an M.A. in Economics and a Ph.D. in Business and Applied Economics from the Wharton School of the University of Pennsylvania.